Legal Almanac Series No. 17

SCHOOLS AND THE LAW

Third Revised Edition

By

E. Edmund Reutter, Jr., Ph. D.

1970
OCEANA PUBLICATIONS, INC.
Dobbs Ferry, New York

This is the seventeenth number in a series of LEGAL ALMANACS which bring you the law on various subjects in nontechnical language. These books do not take the place of your attorney's advice, but they can introduce you to your legal rights and responsibilities.

Library of Congress Catalog Card Number 64-7617
Standard Book Number 379-11067-9
© Copyright 1970 by Oceana Publications, Inc.

TABLE OF CONTENTS

ABOUT THE AUTHOR

E. Edmund Reutter, Jr., Ph.D., is Professor of Education at Teachers College, Columbia University. He is author of *The School Administrator and Subversive Activities* and co-author of *The Law of Public Education, Legal Aspects of School Board Operation, Staff Personnel in the Public Schools,* and *The Yearbook of School Law.* He has served as President of the National Organization on Legal Problems of Education and has contributed numerous articles and chapters to publications in the fields of education and law.

Chapter I

OVERVIEW OF LEGAL FRAMEWORK
FOR THE PUBLIC SCHOOLS

"Today, education is perhaps the most important function of state and local governments. Compulsory school attendance laws and the great expenditures for education both demonstrate our recognition of the importance of education to our democratic society. It is required in the performance of our most basic public responsibilities, even service in the armed forces. It is the very foundation of good citizenship. Today it is a principal instrument in awakening the child to cultural values, in preparing him for later professional training, and in helping him to adjust normally to his environment. In these days, it is doubtful that any child may reasonably be expected to succeed in life if he is denied the opportunity of an education." Thus in 1954 spoke the Supreme Court of the United States.

In the United States, differing from almost every other country of the world, the national government has no direct control or authority in the field of public education. Since education is not mentioned in the federal Constitution, under the Tenth Amendment it becomes one of the powers reserved to the states. The states have established local school districts with boards of education to operate the schools.

The concept of a free public school for all the children, however, was not very well developed when the United States became a nation. Early court decisions influenced a recognition of the legal purpose of the public school as the development of a citizenry capable of participating effectively in self-government. As public education evolved, it became from a legal point of view as much a duty of children

1

to submit to instruction as a right that they had. The right of the government is limited, however, to requiring that children study certain subjects; it cannot demand that all children attend a public school. This is one of many situations involving education in which the rights of the state come into conflict with the rights of individuals, in this instance, parents. The federal Constitution, as interpreted by the Supreme Court, gives to parents the right to select where and how their children are to be educated so long as minimum essentials within the prerogative of the state to establish are observed.

Each state has established a public school system unique in some respects from those in other states. Yet, despite great diversity, often in important items, the similarities among the states on fundamental concepts are striking. The variations are more often those of form, rather than of substance, and more commonly of degree, rather than of basic approach. It becomes obvious from legal study that the states have tremendously influenced one another, and although each has gone its own way, rare is the situation in a state which has no counterpart in other states. Exceptions exist to every attempted generalization; yet frequently "the exceptions tend to prove the rule."

The following chapters are devoted to specific aspects of the law affecting public schools. By "the law" is meant all of the rules and arrangements recognized by the courts. A part of the law is written and available in codified form. There is a hierarchy of "legislation" applying to the public schools. No act of a body lower in the system can be inconsistent with higher authority properly exercised. The federal Constitution heads the list, followed by federal statutes, state constitution, state statutes, regulations of the state-level educational agency, and regulations of local-level school authorities.

Most of the law, however, is not available in a precisely organized pattern. This is the so-called "common law." It is found in court opinions through the years as judges have resolved controversies and recorded their reasoning. It is this part of the law that frequently gives operational meaning to written regulations and that comes into play when written rules do not exist on a point.

In the United States there are two systems of courts: state courts and federal courts. State courts decide most cases involving public education. Some of those involving the United States Constitution are tried in federal courts. Appellate courts exist in each system to consider appeals from decisions of lower courts. Federal courts and the Supreme Court of the United States are becoming increasingly involved in educational matters as more and more litigants claim violations of various rights protected by the federal Constitution.

On the basis of concrete cases decided by courts through the years it is possible to find a degree of guidance as to what the law on an unadjudicated point is likely to be. Predictions are fraught with peril but, as with most things, there are levels of skill based on study and intelligence.

No other function of government has been separated legally from the main stream as has public education. Although generally true on the state level, it is most pronounced on the local level. Public education, almost universally throughout the country, is kept closer to the control of the people than other aspects of government. In about nine of ten school districts in the land the board of education is directly elected by the voters. The common situation is for local voters to elect two governing boards—one for general local government and one for the public schools.

As amplified in subsequent chapters, local boards of education enjoy wide discretionary powers. The states have not, however, relinquished their legal responsibility for education to local units. Local members of school boards are considered to be state, rather than local, officials. School buildings in legal contemplation are state property. Some states have accentuated the uniqueness of the public education function by establishing local school districts with boundaries distinct from municipal divisions. But even where boundaries are the same, school boards to differing extents are independent of control by officers of general government.

Public schools are public in the several senses of being open to all the children, of being financed by public funds, and of being subject to public control of policies. Citizens as individuals and as groups can influence educational policy in ways other than election of board members. Meetings of boards of education generally are open to the public. Regardless, the transactions are of public business, and the records are open to the public. Also, frequently citizens have a direct voice in determining expenditures.

The right of a parent to control the education of his child is deeply engrained in the common law. Judicial precedent dictates that legislation which changes the common law is to be narrowly construed. Parents' rights must yield only where their exercise impairs the general welfare.

From the perspective of the law, perhaps the point at which the individual citizen can exercise most influence is through what is known as a taxpayer's suit. This type of legal action arises when a taxpayer sues on the ground that an action is beyond the power of the body involved or that it represents an abuse of discretion in that a recognized power is being unreasonably or arbitrarily exercised. The element of spending public money generally is present, although in many instances the alleged improper expenditure is somewhat remote from the main issue.

Two of the most common suits broadly affecting educational matters are those where the intent is to require a governmental body or official to carry out a function that is alleged to be a duty, and those where it is sought to halt or to prevent some action that is alleged to be unauthorized by law. The complaint of one taxpayer can be sufficient to activate the courts to examine a situation and to enunciate the law on the point. The fact that the overwhelming majority of affected people may approve a challenged action has no effect on its legality. Neither does the fact that a practice has been unquestioned legally over a long period of years.

The following chapters present the law as it is. There are methods of changing any aspect which is felt to be inconsistent with the best interests of the nation.

Chapter II

THE FEDERAL GOVERNMENT
AND EDUCATION

Despite the fact that education is not mentioned in the Constitution of the United States and, therefore, is not a function of the federal government, that governmental level has exercised considérable influence in the development of the American public school system. This influence has been both direct and indirect and has increased as the years have gone by. The proper role of the federal government in connection with public education has been widely discussed in the past and is of growing importance at the present.

Legislative Branch (Congress)

Congress has exercised over the years much direct influence through its constitutional power "to lay and collect taxes . . . to pay the debts and provide for the common defense and general welfare of the United States." Actually the extent of this power in relation to public education is judicially uncertain. There has been no direct judicial test involving specifically education. However, the interpretations of the Supreme Court of the United States in related areas give rise to the belief that Congress does indeed have the power to provide federal financial aid to education. Also it would appear difficult to argue at the present time that public education is not connected with "the general welfare of the United States" as a whole.

A series of decisions by the Supreme Court of the United States in the 1930's resolved a persistent argument about the federal taxing and spending power in favor of the interpretation that it pertains not only to the specific legislative fields set out for Congress, but to any field that would promote the general welfare. In sustaining the old-age benefits article of the Social Security Act as a permissible area for Congressional spending for the general welfare, the Court said: "The discretion [as to whether a particular expenditure could be justified under the welfare clause], however, is not confided to the courts. The discretion belongs to Congress, unless the choice is clearly wrong, a display of arbitrary power, not an exercise of judgment . . . . Nor is the concept of the general welfare static. Needs that were narrow and parochial a century ago may be interwoven in our day with the well-being of the nation. What is critical or urgent changes with the times."

The first instance of federal-level legislation in the area of the public schools took place even before the federal Constitution was adopted. The Ordinances of 1785 and 1787 provided for land grants to the states from the public domain for the "maintenance of public schools" and stated the policy that "religion, morality, and knowledge being necessary to good government and the happiness of mankind, schools and the means of education shall be forever encouraged." These acts gave impetus to the development of school systems in many states.

The Morrill Act of 1862 was crucial in the founding of the so-called "land-grant" colleges, originally established for the major purpose of teaching agricultural and mechanical arts. In 1917 federal aid to support vocational education in public secondary schools was instituted. In 1946 the federal government enacted the National School Lunch Act which has been instrumental in the development of improved lunch programs for children in non-public as well as public schools. All three of these operations in somewhat modified forms continue to receive financial support from the federal government.

There also have been several instances of Congressional action of a short term nature. During the depression years of the 1930's much federal money was spent on educational activities in connection with such programs as those of the Civilian Conservation Corps and the National Youth Administration. The "G.I. Bill" following World War II and the similar bill following the Korean War provided grants directly to students in connection with their educational programs either in high school or on the college level. Federal aid has been provided for public school education in those communities burdened excessively by increases of enrollments due to concentrations of population brought on by the presence in the area of federal military and defense installations. The 1958 National Defense Education Act was aimed at strengthening certain areas of education. This act provided grants to institutions and students pursuing certain types of programs, chiefly in the areas of foreign languages, mathematics, science, and counseling.

The most comprehensive federal legislation pertaining to the public schools was the Elementary and Secondary Education Act of 1965. This act introduced a new focus for federal money—poverty. Funds were made available to school districts for special programs designed to meet the needs of children in attendance areas containing concentrations of low income families. The act also provided funds for improved instructional materials and for developing innovative ideas.

Furthermore, sight should not be lost of the large sums of money spent by Congress in connection with educational activities not directly associated with the public educational system. Examples include education programs for farmers, immigrants, government employees, members of the Armed Forces, American Indians, and underdeveloped countries.

The issue of federal control is closely tied to federal financial grants. The Supreme Court of the United States has considered cases involving federal regulation or control through taxation of matters reserved to the states (as is education). Such use of federal taxing power has been declared unconstitutional in a series of cases, the best known, perhaps, involving the Agricultural Adjustment Act of 1933. This does not mean, of course, that Congress cannot set up any controls at all. Rather, it means that the primary purpose of the legislation cannot be regulation of such matters.

7

The amount of control exercised by the federal government in its various undertakings affecting education ranges from no regulation or control in the Ordinance of 1785 and almost none in the land-grant college appropriations to more extensive control in connection with vocational education and to virtually complete control in the National Youth Administration Program. Although these acts have not been judicially challenged, it seems apparent that in none was control of education a purpose superseding that of promoting the general welfare.

Congress has also influenced public school education through inquiries and hearings, which have been conducted on several occasions since World War II for the purpose of investigating whether there is need for federal legislation. The most far reaching hearings were those conducted by the House Committee on Un-American Activities and the Senate Judiciary Sub-committee on the subject of subversion in the education process. Investigations conducted by Congress into such areas as student unrest, use of narcotics, and problems of poverty have had an effect on public school educational policies. The fact that education is a state function apparently does not bar Congressional committees from conducting investigations into this area with the rationale that legislation for the general welfare is contemplated.

The failure of Congress to legislate in an area may indirectly affect public education. For example, substantial proportions of state and local school funds were diverted following World War II to pay for school buildings, as distinguished from the instructional program, as an indirect result of a Congressional policy of not affording aid to states for school construction at a time when school age population was rapidly increasing. Inactivity of Congress in the area of civil rights for Negroes has profoundly altered the development of public education. To assess the role of Congress in relation to education, the amount of money placed into a program must be examined as well as the wording of the legislative authorization for the program.

Executive Branch

The executive branch of the federal government is given differing amounts of authority in connection with the administration of the various acts of Congress. The most direct influence on education is exercised in those instances in which the executive branch has the power to approve certain state or local programs before federal money can be forthcoming. Less direct influence emerges from general executive rule-making power in connection with legislation. Educational policy has been affected by reports of White House Conferences and Presidential Advisory Committees set up in connection with general or specific goals of education or with federal relations to the states.

The agency in the executive branch of the federal government which has as its primary function work in the field of public education is the United States Office of Education, located in the Department of Health, Education and Welfare. The United States Office of Education is headed by the United States Commissioner of Education, who is appointed by the President. This office was established by federal statute in 1867 for the purpose of collecting statistics and facts and diffusing information respecting education to "aid the people of the United States in the establishment and maintenance of efficient school systems" and to "otherwise promote the cause of education throughout the country." Thus, its functions are essentially of an advisory nature. Through leadership and service, rather than through authority, this office has exercised varying degrees of influence on American education during its history. Its status was greatly enhanced in the decade of the 1960's, as relatively more federal attention was being given to education.

More programs are being administered through the United States Office of Education, and more authority in the administration of federal grants is being invested in that office. Educators are markedly divided, as are political figures, regarding the appropriate amount of power to place in the Office of Education. The issue involves both that office relative to other offices in the federal government, and that office relative to the states.

It cannot be overemphasized that, except in connection with a federal statute which may vest certain powers in the United States Office of Education in connection with the provisions of that statute, the Office has no authority whatsoever over the conduct of the public schools within the several states.

Judicial Branch

The Supreme Court of the United States has had a far greater influence on the course of public education than is generally realized. Even though education itself is not mentioned in the federal Constitution, many of the amendments to the Constitution involve problems directly associated with it. Also, the provision within the Constitution prohibiting any state from impairing the obligations of a contract has been a factor in many cases involving education which have come before the Supreme Court through the years.

The First Amendment is the legal basis of many issues rather constantly in the courts which may be broadly categorized as church-state-education relationships. Since 1947 the Supreme Court has rendered six highly significant decisions bearing on public policy in this area. The cases have involved sectarian religious instruction within public school buildings, released time during the school day for pupils enrolled in public schools to attend religious instruction outside of the public schools, recitation of prayers and Bible reading in the public schools, and provision of transportation and textbooks at public expense for children attending schools sponsored by religious groups. The Supreme Court found that sectarian instruction within a public school building was a violation of the First Amendment. Released time during the school day for religious instruction outside of the school building, however, was permitted in a subsequent decision. Recitation as part of opening exercises in public schools either of "the Lord's Prayer" or of a prayer which contained the word "God" was banned. So was Bible reading when used for essentially religious purposes. In regard to providing transportation and textbooks at public expense for children attending non-public schools, the Court found no bar in the federal Constitution to such a practice. Therefore, whether there may be a released time program and whether public money may be spent for transportation or textbooks for children in non-public schools are legal decisions to be made within the individual states according to their respective constitutions and statutes. More attention is given to the Supreme Court's church-state-education decisions in Chapter XIV.

The Fourteenth Amendment has been crucial to most of the cases involving education which have been decided by the Supreme Court. The "due process" and "equal protection" concepts have been invoked in cases upholding such diverse rights as the right of teachers to criticize education policies, the right of private schools not to suffer loss of income because of compulsory attendance of children in public schools, the right of parents to have their children study German, and the right of pupils to wear armbands to protest United States foreign policy. It was on Fourteenth Amendment grounds that the Court in 1954 declared unconstitutional pupil assignment policies based on race which were in effect in seventeen states and the District of Columbia. The legal aftermath of the desegregation decision is discussed in Chapter XV.

The Supreme Court's enunciation of the "one man - one vote" rule for elections to state legislatures could have a profound effect on educational policies by changing the compositions, and perhaps the educational attitudes, of most state legislatures. Increasingly attempts are being made to have state and federal courts extend the "one man - one vote" rule to the selection of members of state, county, and local boards of education. (Most local boards have always been chosen in accordance with the principle.) In 1969 the Court struck down a special requirement for voting in school elections in New York, the requirement being essentially that only those who had children in school or who owned or rented real property could vote in such elections.

Chapter III

THE STATE GOVERNMENT AND EDUCATION

Among the fifty states the pattern for the organization and administration of the public schools varies considerably in detail but not in terms of general structure. Except in Hawaii the actual operation of the schools of the state is largely delegated to local boards of education carrying out their functions in school districts set up by the state. On the state level there are three distinguishable components concerned with education. These are: a state board of education, a chief administrative officer, and a state department of education.

The State Board of Education

Although there is variation in terms of power and authority, a state board of education may be described generally as the policy making body for the public schools within a state. It operates just below the state legislature in the legal hierarchy governing education. The state board of education sets up rules and regulations not inconsistent with the constitution and statutes of the state. Such rules and regulations are binding on the local school boards within the state. In two states (Illinois and Wisconsin) there is no single board exercising control over the public schools. (State boards governing institutions of higher education are excluded from this discussion.)

The methods of selection of state board of education members differ from state to state. (See Appendix, Table I.) 112 p. In many states not all members are selected in the same

13

manner. The most frequent mode of selection is that of appointment by the governor. In some states the legislature or a part of it must approve the governor's nomination. Frequently members must meet the qualification of residence within a certain geographic district, and often a maximum age is specified.

At the end of World War II there were no elected state boards, but there has been a trend toward popular election of board members since then. In some states the members are elected on a district basis and in others on a statewide basis. Indirect election is practised in New York, where the members of the state board (Board of Regents) are selected by the state legislature; in Washington, where they are selected by vote of the local school boards; and in South Carolina, where they are selected by legislative delegations.

There has been a marked trend away from what at one time was a common method of obtaining members of state boards of education, that of designating persons occupying other positions in state government as state board members. Some state boards still contain voting ex officio members. Two states (Mississippi and Florida) have state boards entirely comprising this type of member, and one (North Dakota) has ex officio members occupying a majority of the seats on the board.

The Chief State School Officer

Each of the states has a chief administrative officer for the state school system. Different titles for the office are found from state to state, the two most common titles being State Superintendent of Education and State Commissioner of Education. At the end of World War II two-thirds of the chief state school officers were popularly elected, and only eight were selected by state boards of education. Now approximately half of the chief state school officers are selected by state boards. Most of the other half are popularly elected. A few are appointed by governors. (See Appendix, Table II.)

The responsibilities and the authority of the chief state

school officer vary markedly among the states. Often some duties are found in the state constitution and some others are specified by statute. The chief state school officer executes the plans and policies of the state board of education as well as the statutes of the state pertaining to public school education. In every state the chief state school officer is the executive head of the state department of education. He is generally recognized as the educational spokesman for, and coordinator of, the public school enterprise in the state as a whole.

Quite frequently certain judicial functions regarding public educational activities are assigned to the chief state school officer, and certain types of controversies and disputes may or must be submitted to him for disposition. A few states by statute and several by court interpretation require that the chief state school officer give an opinion on certain matters before courts will consider the cases. Of course, once this officer has given an opinion on the matter, the aggrieved party may try to have a court of competent jurisdiction review his decision. Since the chief state school officer is an administrative official, his actions would always be subject to judicial review if it could be substantially alleged that they were contrary to law, were arbitrary, or were beyond his power.

New York has gone further than any other state in vesting judicial powers in the state commissioner of education. The pertinent statute indicates that "any person conceiving himself aggrieved" in a matter "pertaining to common schools" may appeal to the commissioner, whose decision "shall be final and conclusive, and not subject to question or review in any place or court whatever." Despite such a legislative statement the courts of New York have not considered themselves disqualified from considering cases where it is reasonably alleged that the commissioner acted beyond the scope of powers of his administrative office. Also it becomes ultimately the prerogative of the courts to decide the often unclear question of whether a particular matter is a "legal" one or an "administrative" one.

Many cases have arisen in which local parties have objected to the exercise of some power by the chief state school officer. Often the issue is whether a matter delegated to the chief state school officer by the legislature or the state board of education has been accompanied by sufficient guidelines and criteria so as not to constitute an illegal delegation of the legislative prerogative. A number of cases recently have revolved around the accreditation of schools. It has been held that the state commissioner of education does not have the power to determine which schools may and which may not be accredited in the absence of sufficiently directive criteria established in the legislation authorizing him to perform such a function. This question, it should be emphasized, is not one of abuse of discretionary power, but one of whether a power can legally be given to an administrative officer. The line between authority which is delegable and that which is not is very thin. The chief state school officer cannot "legislate," but he can formulate reasonable rules and regulations to implement legislation.

Methods of enforcement of rules and regulations of the state board of education or the state commissioner of education are rather confused in many states. In several jurisdictions it is not clear what can be done to a district or to an individual who does not comply with a state-level rule or regulation. In many states it is possible for state financial aid to be withheld from the local district as a penalty. This type of penalty against a district, however, is often not effective in that those who suffer are the children of the district rather than those who have disobeyed the regulations. In some states the chief state school officer or the state board of education has the power to levy taxes which a local board has refused to do. Also in some states local board members can be removed from office by state authorities. The foregoing applies to instances where criminal violations have not occurred. Penalties for criminal acts are always specified by statute.

The State Department of Education

Each state has a state department of education that includes specialists and professional workers for carrying out the various educational functions to be performed on the state level. State departments of education uniformly are assigned operational responsibility for seeing that school laws are observed. Such items as teacher certification and distribution of state financial grants are handled by these departments. This state of function may be regarded as the regulatory type which by its nature must be performed in every state, although some state departments are more efficient than others due perhaps more to quantity of staff than to quality of individual employees.

Another type of function performed by state departments of education might be characterized as advisement and consultation, the giving of assistance to local school districts with problems in such areas as personnel policies, curriculum, law, and building planning. Frequently local school districts are not in a position to hire expert help in these matters and would not have the advantage of it were it not provided through the state department of education.

Many materials can be prepared on the state level under the auspices of the state department more expeditiously than in the various school districts. In some cases these matterials are imposed upon the local districts and must be observed and followed. In other instances they are merely suggestive or advisory.

State departments of education perform to differing extents the function of coordinating the activities of local school districts in the best interests of the children of the state as a whole. Good practices developed in one school district can be disseminated to other districts through the department.

Each state department of education conducts some research. This ranges from gathering data and statistics on the status quo to analyses of needs and the conducting of experiments designed to help solve educational problems for the state as a whole. Information so obtained is made available to local school districts to utilize as they see fit.

One section of the Elementary and Secondary Education Act of 1965 was focused on strengthening state departments of education. Grants were given for planning, developing, or improving state-level educational operations.

Intermediate Units

About three-fourths of the states have an administrative unit standing between the local school board and the state department of education. The most common basis for establishing intermediate units is the county. Although in these states the large school districts normally communicate directly with the state educational agencies, for certain functions the smaller school districts operate through intermediate units. In some states the intermediate unit is essentially an administrative agency processing reports and checking that certain state requirements are met by local districts. In other states — and this is the emerging concept for the intermediate unit — through the intermediate unit, services of which the following are typical are provided to local school districts: testing and counselling; help with gifted, retarded, and handicapped children; film and record libraries; trade and industrial education; architectural help.

Such facilities normally could not be provided within small school districts for financial reasons or because in some instances there would not be enough work to occupy full-time specialists in these areas. A shared-service operation set up on the intermediate level makes it possible for small school districts to obtain the services of, for example, a school psychologist for one or two days a week. Expenses of such services usually are prorated among participating districts on a basis of benefits received.

About one-fourth of the states operate on what is known as a "county unity" system. In these states the local school district which operates the schools is coterminous with the county, and there are only two governmental levels related to public education within these states—the state level and

18

the county level. Except in West Virginia and Florida, large cities are exempted from the county unit plan.

Local School Districts

It has already been noted that the state has within its power the general right to create, alter, or dissolve school districts as it deems best for the overall educational interests of the state. Local district boundaries may or may not coincide with municipal boundaries.

Recently there has been a wave of concern for the elimination of school districts too small to afford the kind of education deemed necessary for modern times. Although the consolidation of school districts is essentially a political issue rather than a legal issue, some legal points are involved. For example, the impairment of obligations of contracts when districts are altered violates the federal Constitution. This question often arises in connection with the bonded indebtedness of a district. When the boundaries of a district are changed, the amount of taxable property is readjusted possibly to the disadvantage of some bondholders of the original district. Usually laws covering consolidation of districts make some provision for the distribution of debts which may have been incurred by districts being altered. Where the distribution is equitable and not in violation of a constitutional prescription, courts have sustained such statutes. Whether a distribution is indeed equitable becomes a question of fact to be decided in each case.

An even more recent development has been concern for the decentralization of very large school districts. It appears that in the decade of the 1970's as much attention will be given to breaking down such districts as had been given in the preceding two decades to consolidating small districts. Although the basic legal aspects would be little different, political considerations and long established operational traditions and practices make the subdividing of the large districts much more difficult. Problems of finance and personnel administration are particularly perplexing in decentralizing large cities.

Chapter IV

THE LOCAL BOARD OF EDUCATION

The public schools are operated in forty-nine of the fifty states by local boards of education. (Hawaii has one state-wide school district.) The total number of local school districts is approximately twenty thousand. The individual states contain a range from seventeen in Nevada to about fifteen hundred in Nebraska. It should be emphasized that even though education is legally a function of the state, historically it was on the local level that public schools received their impetus. Most states were not in a position to exercise much effective control or leadership on the state level until considerably after public schools were flourishing in many local districts.

Members

The affairs of each local school district are managed by a board of education. Most boards have five, seven, or nine members. These board members legally are regarded as state, rather than local, officials. This is true even in those school districts where boundaries are coterminous with those of municipalities, and where the mayor appoints the members of the board of education. In most districts there is no compensation for board members, although there is reimbursement for expenses. Provision is made for overlapping terms of office in almost all of the school districts of the United States.

Close to 90% of all school board members in the country are popularly elected. (See Appendix, Table III.) Of these most are elected on a non-partisan basis. In about three districts of five, school board elections are held at a time different from elections for other offices in the government.

About a third of the states have statutes specifically stating that all school board elections must be held separately. Most school board members are chosen from the district at large, although in some instances they are chosen on an area basis.

Some statements regarding the qualifications required for membership on local school boards are found in the laws of almost all states. The qualifications, however, are not very restrictive. The most common stipulation is that board members be qualified voters. This would generally include certain age and length of residence aspects. A small number of states have requirements that board members be either taxpayers or parents. Only a few states make reference to educational qualifications, and these are of the order of a "common school education" or "ability to read and write." Thus, from a practical point of view there are almost no restrictions as to which residents of a district may be elected to serve on the board of education.

The manner of choosing local school board members is the prerogative of the legislature, subject, of course, to any state constitutional limitations. Recent Supreme Court pronouncements relative to "one man - one vote" may affect the selection of members of those relatively few local boards where the principle is not already in effect. Definitely unconstitutional, according to the Supreme Court in a 1969 decision, are the requirements then existing in a few states that only property owners, lessees, and parents or guardians of school children could vote in school elections.

A school board member cannot hold an office which is incompatible with his role on the local board of education. Two offices are incompatible when one office is subordinate to the other and the holder of one office would be unable to perform properly his duties under that position without coming into conflict with his duties under the other office. Obviously a school board member could not be an employee of that board. Further, a school board member generally could not in his private capacity do business with the board of education. Many states have statutes that definitely establish or disestablish incompatibility of certain offices and that clarify issues of "conflict of interest."

Powers

IN GENERAL: Local boards of education are regarded as quasi-municipal corporations. Although they have many characteristics of incorporated local governmental bodies such as cities, their powers are much more restricted in that their functions relate only to education. From a practical point of view the differences between a quasi-municipal corporation and a municipal corporation are unimportant; indeed, some courts refer to school boards as municipal corporations. Thus, the common law governing municipal corporations would apply to the government of school districts except where statutes make distinctions.

All authority of a local school board lies with the board as a corporate body. The board is a legal entity distinct from the individuals composing it. A change, therefore, in membership does not change the legal status of the board. A local board of education can enter into binding agreements extending for a reasonable period of time beyond the terms of individual members.

Members of boards of education have no more authority over the schools as individuals than does any citizen. As individuals or as groups, however, they may be delegated certain responsibilities for investigating and recommending action to the board as a whole. One or more members may carry out certain ministerial functions, but discretionary functions must be executed by the board as a whole. A ministerial function is essentially one that involves no choice as to whether or not the function should be performed and generally no option as to how it is to be performed. Obviously the distinction between ministerial and discretionary functions is frequently not clear, and often has to be resolved by courts.

Local boards of education within a state have only those powers which are specifically granted to them by the state constitution and statutes and those powers which are necessarily implied from the express powers. It would appear that this firmly rooted legal definition of school board authority is a rather narrow and confining one. An examination of the cases, however, indicates that most courts have been very liberal in construing the powers "necessarily implied" by the express powers. The local autonomy that is characteristic of American education is as much a result of judicial interpretation as it is of explicit statutory authority granted by the legislatures to local school boards.

Every state has some statutes related to the powers and duties of local boards of education. In some states the statutes are relatively specific, at least in regard to certain items. In others they are quite general. The only way in which powers of a local board can be increased beyond those expressly stated or considered implied by an appropriate court is through legislative action. The legislature may change the powers of local boards of education more or less at its pleasure. It is not necessary that all boards of education within a state have like powers so long as the powers of any school boards in a clear-cut classification are granted to all boards in that group. In most states larger school districts have some powers not afforded smaller school districts.

A local board of education may not refuse to act on a matter covered by mandatory state law. If compliance with the provisions of a statute requires the expenditure of money, it is incumbent upon the local board to raise the money in an appropriate manner. In those districts where local boards do not have the power to raise money themselves but must obtain the money from some municipal agency, that agency must furnish the funds necessary for the board to comply with all state statutes.

It is important to distinguish between a board's exceeding its power and a board's abusing its discretion. Many cases revolve about the question of whether a local board of education has the power to do something. If it is found that the board does indeed have the power, then there may follow the subsequent question as to whether the board has abused its discretion in exercising the power. The legal rule is that where it is not clear that a local agency has a power, the issue should be resolved against the grant of power. But it is also the general rule that where a governmental body has the discretion to do something, it is assumed that the discretion has not been abused, and the burden of proof is on the party contending that an action constitutes an abuse of discretion.

The courts will not substitute their judgment for that of the local board of education in matters involving discretion. That is to say, courts will not pass upon the wisdom of a local board action when the board has the power to perform the action in question. The courts will, however, check that the board does not act arbitarily or unreasonably in carrying out its discretionary functions. Where local boards of education act unwisely, resource is at the polls, not in the courts. The courts will intervene through a properly instituted lawsuit, however, if a board of education has acted unreasonably and therefore has abused its discretion. Reasonableness of a board action is a question of law to be determined in each instance by the court; it is not a matter of fact for jury determination. An action can be unreasonable in terms of subject matter or in terms of method of implementation or enforcement.

Much of the material covered in subsequent chapters pertains to specific powers of local boards of education.

CONTRACTUAL POWERS: The authority of a local board of education to enter into contracts is governed to some extent by statute. Contracts not made according to statutory prescriptions are not valid. If contracts of employment must be in writing, an oral contract with a teacher cannot be honored, or if contracts for the purchase of certain kinds of equipment must be awarded to the lowest responsible bidder, a contract not so let will be invalid.

Embedded in the common law is the concept that contractors with public bodies enter into the contracts at their own peril. The rationale is that the powers of public bodies are known to all (since they are contained in public documents), and it is not in the public interest to hold taxpayers financially responsible for illegal agreements made by public officers. Further, were these officers to be held personally liable if they were unexpert in the law, it would be impossible to get good men in public office because of the inordinate risk.

Generally, if a school board enters into a contract that turns out not to be valid, neither the school district nor individual members can be held liable. For example, a contractor cannot force a school district to carry out a contract the execution of which would require expenditures beyond its debt limit, despite the fact that in all other respects the contract was valid. Also, he would be barred from recovery of damages from individual board members. A major exception to this rule is if there has been fraud or misrepresentation on the part of school board members in obtaining the contract. In some jurisdictions criminal penalties accrue if school board members make certain types of illegal contracts, for example, with themselves or with close relatives.

There are many instances where local boards of education enter into contracts which they have the authority to make, but which are improper due to failure to observe some technicality. It is the general rule in such situations that this type of agreement can be made into a valid contract if the board of education so desires. It may be validated by taking the action which was not taken at the time the agreement was entered into. If, as illustration, a certain kind of contract must be made by a roll call vote of the members of the board of education and no roll call was taken when the contract was awarded, the board can validate it by a roll call vote at a subsequent meeting.

Procedures

MEETINGS: In order for an action of a board of education to be binding, the action must be taken at an official meeting. Although this seems obvious, much litigation revolves about the question of whether a particular meeting was actually a legal one. Many states have statutes governing certain aspects of the problem, but a large proportion of the cases are resolved by courts according to the common law.

Board meetings may be classified as regular or special. Regular meetings are definitely scheduled well in advance and are for handling general school board business. Special meetings are those called at irregular times usually for special purposes. For an action at a special meeting to be legally binding, all board members must have had adequate notice that such a meeting would be held. In some states the purpose of the meeting must be specified in the notice.

In the absence of a statute to the contrary, a quorum (the number of board members who must be present when business is transacted) is a majority of the authorized membership. Business of the school district can be transacted by a majority of a quorum under the common law. Frequently statutes specify that certain types of business require the affirmative action of a larger proportion of board membership. For example, a majority of the entire board (rather than a majority of those present) may have to vote in favor of employing someone related to a board member.

Statutory procedures must be followed at board meetings or actions taken may be held invalid. A board of education has the power to adopt its own rules of procedure so long as these are not in conflict with any laws. The courts will hold local boards to compliance with their own rules once adopted.

It should be noted that official action must be taken at an official meeting. Even if every board member has individually approved something, only at a properly called meeting of the board as a whole can the action be made legally effective.

HEARINGS: Before taking certain types of actions school boards must hold hearings. This is most frequently the case in connection with the dismissal of a teacher serving under a tenure statute. However, the necessity of a hearing may also arise by implication from a statute providing that a particular action be taken only for cause, as the board has to determine whether the cause actually exists. It should be emphasized, however, that not all board actions must be preceded by hearings. The holding of a fairly conducted hearing, however, is evidence to the effect that a board of education has indeed considered a matter rather than having acted arbitrarily.

In many instances statutes cover the procedure to be followed in hearings, and in others local boards have adopted their own rules of procedure in hearings. In either case the rules must be carefully followed in order for the hearing to fulfill legal requirements.

When the hearing involves the dismissal of a teacher, the general requirements of "due process" must be observed. Precisely what these are is a matter for court determination in individual situations. Procedures related to the dismissal of teachers under tenure statutes are further discussed in Chapter VIII.

RECORDS: There is variation among the states regarding the records that school boards must keep. The official records of a board of education are prima facie evidence of actions taken and thus are of great importance. Where statutes require records of proceedings to be kept, generally oral or other evidence is inadmissible to contradict the official record. The judicial rule that excludes other evidence to alter official records is subject to certain exceptions in individual cases. As illustration, when the minutes are not clear or are indefinite, other evidence must be considered in order that justice be done. If there is an error in the record, the remedy is to have it corrected at an appropriate meeting.

Since the board of education is a public body, its records are considered public documents. This means that any taxpayer has a right to examine the records of the board of education. The taxpayer does not have the right to do so at his convenience. The board of education has the responsibility for making the records available reasonably soon after a meeting has been completed and during reasonable times of day. It has been held not necessary that minutes of a meeting be approved at a subsequent board of education meeting before a taxpayer has a right to examine them. The minutes do not constitute an official record, however, until approved in the prescribed manner.

Chapter V

DETERMINING WHAT IS TAUGHT

State Requirements

Almost complete power over what must be taught and what must not be taught lies with the state legislature. The only checks are the individual liberties protected by the federal Constitution and its amendments and any provisions or restrictions which may be found in the state constitution. In some states there are a large number of statutes pertaining directly to the curriculum. In others there are relatively few detailed laws. Also varying among the states is the degree of coverage of rules and regulations of state boards and state departments of education. In all states, however, operationally it is the local board of education which has the most to say about what is taught to the boys and girls in the public schools. Even where certain subjects must be taught, the methods of teaching essentially become a matter of local determination.

A few state constitutions contain provisions regarding what is taught. The Constitution of Utah, for example, requires teaching of the metric system. The most frequent provisions in state constitutions affecting the curriculum treat the area of church and state relationships. Teaching the Constitution of the United States is required by statute in almost all states. About two-thirds of the states require teaching the appropriate state constitution. Three states out of four require the teaching of the history of our country in elementary grades, and some 19 states do so in high school. Other common curricular mandates include instruction in such items as arithmetic, spelling, effects of alcohol and narcotics, conservation, health, safety, and physical training. The observance in the public schools of such holidays as

Washington's Birthday and Armistice Day is commonly prescribed. Some detail on the observance is often included in laws or state level administrative provisions. Delaware law, for example, specifies that exercises be held "between the hours of eleven A.M. and twelve o'clock noon in memory of 'Armistice Day'."

Many laws go further than stating what subjects should be taught and indicate the grades in which each should be taught and sometimes how many hours should be devoted to the subject. Indiana, as illustration, prescribes that "five full recitation periods of class discussion" concerning elections be given for all pupils in grades 6 through 12 within the two weeks immediately preceding certain election days.

Some states include in their statutes provisions that certain subjects must be taught if prescribed numbers of voters petition for them. Other laws require that local boards of education permit children to be excused from some activities for given reasons. For example, laws requiring the teaching of hygiene and sanitary science sometimes exempt from certain aspects of the subject those children whose parents object on religious grounds.

Many states have statutes which go beyond the establishment of certain fields of knowledge that must be taught and move into the area of ideas and attitudes. "Patriotism" and "good citizenship" are illustrations of attitudes which must be taught in many states. Nebraska adds a negative twist and requires teaching of "opposition to all organizations and activities that would destroy our present form of government." Several states require instruction in the area of moral conduct. Florida law directs teachers to inculcate "principles of truth and honesty" as well as "the practice of every Christian virtue." Judicial doctrines arising primarily in the 1960's raise questions as to the enforceability of such vague prescriptions.

Of rather recent origin are statutes requiring the establishment of classes for "handicapped" children. Types of physical disabilities usually are listed, as are "I.Q." levels for "educable" and "trainable" children. Often special state funds are provided for extra costs of such classes.

Many states still require the flag salute and the pledge of allegiance despite the fact that Supreme Court of the United States has ruled that such an exercise cannot be made compulsory. The Supreme Court, it should be noted, ruled that a child could not be compelled to salute the flag against his parent's wishes; the Court did not rule that the ritual was unconstitutional as an element in the public school program. This situation illustrates one facet of the law pertaining to "required" subjects or activities in public schools.

The courts consistently have held that subjects essential to good citizenship may be required of all students regardless of parental wishes. Subjects not essential to good citizenship may be required as conditions for academic recognition, such as, passing from grade to grade and receiving a diploma, but not as conditions for remaining in school or for avoiding punitive actions by school authorities. Unreasonableness is the basis for challenging this latter type of requirement. The courts rely heavily on expert opinion of educators as to the reasonableness of such requirements, and the burden of proof of unreasonableness rests on the complaining parent. It should be observed, however, that recently courts have shown a greater disposition to question more rigorously the validity of requirement which are alleged to infringe basic constitutional rights.

If a child refuses at his parent's request to participate in a particular curricular activity, school authorities may do one of three things: they may accede to the request, they may take disciplinary action against the offender, or they may take academic action against the offender. Parents' rights in the education of their children are discussed in Chapter VII and punishments in Chapter IX.

State Prohibitions

As the state may require that certain things be taught, so may it prohibit teachings which can be shown to be inimical to the best interests of the state in general, or to the health, safety, or morals of the people of the state. Polygamy is an example of a teaching held improper regardless of statute.

The most common items which by statute specifically may not be taught are "sectarian" doctrines, "subversive" doctrines, Communism, and vivisection.

It seems clear today that in the context of enforceable prohibitions, "teach" connotes such sense as "state as a fact," "state without indicating that there are other points of view," or "urge that a pupil accept;" rather than "mention," "discuss," or "state as an opinion of the teacher."

Two decisions of the United States Supreme Court bear on the matter of the state's power to prohibit specific teachings in schools. In 1923 the Court set up as a condition for barring a teaching in a private school the showing of a type of harm which could result from the teaching and which the state would have a right to prevent. The particular case involved a Nebraska statute which provided that a foreign language must not be taught in a grade lower than the ninth, the purpose of the statute allegedly being to help develop good American citizens. The Court held that such a statute infringed the right of language teachers to carry on their profession, the right of parents to direct the education of their children, and the right of pupils to acquire knowledge.

In 1968, the Supreme Court invalidated an Arkansas statute prohibiting the teaching of the theory of evolution in public schools. The basis of that decision was a finding that the statute violated the constitutional prohibition against laws respecting the establishment of religion because the statute was enacted to further a particular religious view.

SECTARIAN TEACHINGS: Frequently prohibitions against the teaching of sectarian doctrines are contained in general constitutional or statutory statements covering relations between the state and the church. About a dozen state constitutions specifically bar sectarian instruction in the public schools of those states. Statutes of some thirteen states forbid the use in public schools of books or pamphlets favoring any particular sect.

The 1963 decision of the Supreme Court ruling out Bible reading as part of opening exercises probably affected at least as many school districts as did the desegregation decision of 1954. Statutes requiring or permitting Bible reading in public schools existed in about one-third of the states. Local boards in many others utilized the procedure without specific statutory authorization, and the practice had been upheld by some courts.

Although no state constitution or statute had expressly forbidden Bible reading, courts in some states had barred it. Also, most of the state courts which had upheld the practice, especially in more recent times, had pointed out that an individual pupil could not be forced under peril of punishment to attend the Bible reading exercise.

The United States Supreme Court decision regarding the Bible did not rule out the Bible as a work of literature or as an historical document. It does seem clear, however, that public schools cannot give Bible instruction in the religious sense.

The distribution of Gideon Bibles to public school students whose parents indicated they wanted the Bibles was held by the Supreme Court of New Jersey in 1953 to be contrary to the principle of separation of church and state. The court noted that not all groups accepted the teachings of the Gideon Bible. It ruled that this Bible was in the category of sectarian literature, and distribution of it through the schools constituted a preference of one religion over another. The Supreme Court of the United States declined to review this decision. More recently a Florida appeals court followed the New Jersey view.

A 1952 decision of the Supreme Court of New Mexico forbid the distribution through the schools of religious pamphlets. Although the teacher did not hand them to the pupils, or even tell the pupils to take or read them, the booklets were kept in sight of the pupils and supplies were replenished when diminished.

The use of prayers in public schools was invalidated by the United States Supreme Court in 1962 as regards a prayer mentioning God (which had been intended by the state board of education to be denominationally neutral) and in 1963 as regards the Lord's Prayer. The facts that teachers do not comment and that pupils are excused at their parent's request do not render prayer recitation constitutional, for the process of selecting and saying the prayer was held to constitute an establishment of religion in the First Amendment sense. Prohibited by a subsequent federal Court of Appeals ruling was the recitation by children of a prayer-like verse before eating in school.

The wearing of distinctive religious garb by teachers has been litigated in state courts on several occasions through the years. The leading case was in 1894 in Pennsylvania where the court held that wearing of religious dress was not in itself a sectarian influence which fell under constitutional bans. However when the legislature the following year enacted a statute forbidding teachers from wearing any religious insignia, the court found the statute to be constitutional. A few states have such statutes, and those which have been challenged in the courts have been sustained. Membership in a religious order, however, has been held not to make one ineligible for public school employment.

SUBVERSIVE TEACHINGS: By the early 1950's approximately two-thirds of the states had specific legislation aimed at controlling subversive teachings. Such teachings were defined or described in various ways as being related to the overthrow of the government by unconstitutional means. Some of the statutes prescribed oaths whereby teachers pledged not to teach subversive doctrines; others barred such teachings explicity without requiring oaths. Some states had both types of statute. When challenged, most of the statutes were judicially sustained through the 1950's. There was a marked reversal in judicial thinking, however, in the decade of the 1960's. By the end of that decade many statutes had been declared unconstitutional, with the judicial reasoning utilized casting doubt over the enforceability of many of the remaining statutes.

This matter is discussed further in Chapter VIII. Pertinent here, however, is the observation that no court has suggested that a state does not have a right to protect itself against the teaching in public schools of truly subversive doctrines. The constitutional infirmities found were in the way the stricken statutes were written and applied.

State Guides

In most instances the number of elements which must be taught and which must not be taught in the public schools of a state is very small compared to all the curricular offerings in the typical public school. States have gone to varying lengths to set up guides to help local school boards provide appropriate curricula for the schools under their jurisdictions. In some cases these guides must be followed and in others they are entirely suggestive to local school officials and teachers.

States departments of education frequently prepare courses of study in various subjects, lists of teaching aids, lists of readings, and the like. State departments also generally employ experts in various aspects of the curriculum. These personnel frequently direct conferences which are designed to help local districts develop their educational programs. Also they may be made available directly to local districts on request for assistance in solving local curricular problems. Consultants employed on the state level are increasing in number in most states as state-level educational agencies evolve from essentially a regulatory role to a true leadership role in improving the quality of education within their borders.

Local Determinations

The local board of education is bound to follow state level prescriptions related to the curriculum. These include statutes, state board of education regulations, rules of the chief state school officer, and judicial interpretations thereof. The fact that the local board of education or local citizens disagree with a state mandate is not sufficient excuse for failure to comply with the state requirement. For example, if a statute stipulates that upon the petition of a given number of parents of children attending a school a subject must be offered in the curriculum, a local board must act on the basis of a valid petition. If a state syllabus is prescribed for a subject, it must be followed by the local authorities regardless of their views on the matter. Even where funds are not readily available locally to support a required activity, courts have held that sufficient money must be raised to carry it on.

Since the local board of education is the legal body most closely connected with what is taught boys and girls, operationally it has vast powers for determining the curriculum. The history of innovations in the curriculum of public schools in the United States is largely a history of local actions. That is to say, a curricular change conceived and initiated by a local board of education which proves successful is copied in other districts and gradually finds its way into general acceptance. Such development may be fostered by a permissive or a mandatory state law. In many instances, however, there is no firm legislative basis for performing a particular curricular activity which has become generally accepted. Among the offerings of most public schools today which originated in the aforementioned way are many athletic activities, kindergartens, dramatics, music, and domestic science, as well as the high school as an outgrowth of the "common school." Analysis of court holdings leads to the generalization that in modern times so long as local boards of education do not go exceedingly far, the addition of courses or activities will be upheld by courts. Indeed, innovations are being less frequently challenged as time passes.

Although it can be stated that the courts have been especially liberal in interpreting the discretionary powers of local boards of education acting with good motivation, it would be unwise to believe that such discretion is unlimited. For example, as regards the establishment of junior colleges in the absence of specific legislative authority to do so, the courts are divided. Also courts have set up limits on activities of certain kinds. As illustration, school health programs including physical examinations are legally sound, but furnishing treatment for deficiences noted has been judicially disapproved. The one major exception is in the area of first aid or emergency treatment.

Furthermore, because a certain function needs to be performed in the general public interest by some governmental agency does not necessarily mean that the school is the governmental vehicle for its performance. Precisely where the powers of the local school board stop and those of other state and local agencies begin is a point not established clearly in the law.

Just as the local board of education has wide powers in establishing new courses of study and activities, so has it the power to alter and even to drop activities and courses which are not required by the state. In the absence of statutes to the contrary, the fact that a large number of parents desire a course to be offered has no legal bearing on whether the local board of education complies with the request. The remedy of parents who want their children to study a subject which the board of education does not approve is to secure a state mandate on the point (that is, a statute or a regulation of the state board of education), to persuade the board through logical or political means to adopt the course, or to elect new members to the board of education.

Chapter VI

DETERMINING HOW IT IS TAUGHT

Many states have statutes pertaining to how prescribed elements in the public school curriculum are taught. Some treat methodology in general and others specifically relate to books and materials used for instructional purposes.

Methods of Instruction

Generally speaking, methods of instruction are chiefly within the province of local school authorities and individual teachers. Often a state statute requiring that a certain element be taught goes farther and indicates some mandates or suggestions as to how it should be taught. For examples, it is commonly indicated that the bad effects of alcohol and narcotics should receive the emphasis of the instruction; Florida law states that prescribed subjects be taught "by means of pictures, charts, oral instruction and lectures, and other approved methods"; Minnesota teachers must encourage patriotism by "readings from American history and from the biographies of American statesmen and patriots." Also, through textbooks, discussed in the next section, a certain degree of influence over methods may be applied by the state.

About two thirds of the states provide that all instruction in the public schools be given in the English tongue. Louisiana has such a provision in the state constitution. Many of the statutes make exceptions for those children of foreign parents who could not profit from instruction in English. Even if a statute does not make such exceptions, it is clear that local boards may make temporary provisions to instruct children in their native tongues until they can become proficient enough in English to understand instruction in that medium.

Perhaps the area in which methods have come into most frequent litigation in recent years involves the inculcation of moral values. The Supreme Court of the United States has held unconstitutional the bringing into the public school of religious leaders for the purpose of giving instruction during the school day to children whose parents so requested. On the other hand, excusing children from the school for an hour per week to attend sectarian religious instruction when so requested by their parents was sustained by the United States Supreme Court as not being in violation of church and state provisions of the First Amendment to the federal Constitution.

The legal situation involving use of the Bible in public schools is treated in Chapters V and XIV. Since the 1963 decision of the Supreme Court on the specific point of use of the Bible in opening exercises, various states and local school districts are reassessing their methods of using the Bible in public schools. It seems clear that the public schools cannot give instruction in the Bible as a means of teaching good citizenship or morality. The Bible, however, may be used in classes in literature and history as a literary or historical document, as distinguished from a religous document. Whether religious hymns may be sung apparently depends upon the setting in which the hymns are used; that is to say, if they are used as examples of certain types of music, or are used from a cultural rather than a religious point of view, they are legally acceptable.

References to the Deity in ceremonial or patriotic exercises are not barred by the federal Constitution. Thus the Pledge of Allegiance does not offend the Constitution. On the other hand, the Supreme Court has expressly declared that one may not be required to salute the flag, even if such is intended as a method of teaching patriotism. The highest court has held that the constitutional liberties of the individual are paramount to the interests of the state in regard to this symbolic patriotic gesture. Although the pupil's reason for not saluting the flag in that case was a religious one, the opinion of the Court indicated that some reasons other than those based on religious grounds might be acceptable.

State departments of education in required or suggested course syllabi frequently treat methods as well as content. Local school boards are vested with discretionary power to authorize or prohibit within broad limits certain methods. Of course, the determination of methods in any field is basically a question for professional competence.

The courts are reluctant to interfere with methods used in public schools. Only where individual rights are abused or where marked arbitrariness of school personnel is apparent will they step in as a rule. Nor are parents the ones to decide methods of instruction, according to the weight of judicial authority. Of course, in some factual situations parents' objections have prevailed. The overall rule, however, is that the school authorities have the legal power to prescribe the methods to be used, and although parents may have the right to withdraw their children from certain classes where they object to the methods, they do not have the right to assert positively methods that must or must not be followed.

Textbooks

All states have some legislation relating to textbooks in public schools. There is no question as to the legal right of a state to prescribe textbooks. The power has been sustained uniformly as an aspect of the state's recognized basic control over education. There is, however, wide variation among the states in implementation of this legal authority.

In about half of the states textbook selection is controlled either by the state board of education or by a special state textbook commission. In those states having a state textbook commission the members generally are connected professionally with public education. For a given subject or a given grade the state may prescribe a single book, or there may be a list of several from which local authorities may choose. The prescription of a single textbook which must be used in all classes in a given subject throughout the state is almost

41

non-existent today, the trend being toward the establishment on the state level of multiple lists of books.

In the other half of the states the local school board is given almost complete authority to select the textbooks for the children within the school district. Moreover, even in those states requiring mandatory use of textbooks selected by state-level agencies, local boards of education have the authority to utilize supplementary books. Also, they have authority to select textbooks for courses offered locally that are not required by the state.

In a few states, for example, Colorado and Utah, there are constitutional prescriptions prohibiting the legislature and state board of education from prescribing textbooks. In most states where the matter is handled locally, the delegation of authority to local boards is statutory. It should be noted, however, that textbook selection performed locally does not mean that the state cannot assert its powers when it so desires.

It is interesting to note that the basic pattern of textbook selection within individual states has changed relatively little in the last several decades. There is no tendency structurally either to centralize or to decentralize the function, although within the basic structure of state-level selection there is discernible a tendency to give more leeway to local boards of education.

Many states have laws regulating relations of school authorities with textbook publishers. This is true even in some states where local school boards adopt books. For example, publishers may be required to list their textbooks and the prices for them with some state official. Most of these states then require that the prices charged within the state be no higher than those charged in any other jurisdiction. Some states have statutes to the effect that once a book has been adopted as a text it cannot be changed by a local board for a specific number of years.

Not uncommon are statutes treating the content of textbooks. Passages of a subversive nature often are specifically barred, as is sectarian material. Texas law furnishes an example of another type of prescription: "All textbooks on physiology and hygiene purchased in the future for use in the public schools of this State shall include at least one chapter on the effects of alcohol and narcotics."

In over two-thirds of the states textbooks are provided free to students in at least some grades. In about half of these states the books are paid for by state, rather than local, funds. Statutes in some states provide that textbooks be furnished to children who do not attend public schools. Such statutes have been found by the Supreme Court of the United States not to violate the federal Constitution if sectarian volumes are not supplied.

Materials

Selection of materials of instruction other than textbooks generally is left to the discretion of local school authorities. State-level prohibitions, such as on sectarian and subversive materials, would of course prevail.

Most states have statutes authorizing local boards to purchase certain types of items which are necessary for the conduct of the school, such as, furniture, laboratory apparatus, stationery supplies, and chalkboards. Some of these laws are not very clear. Also new curricular patterns require differing equipment. The courts in general have accorded local school boards wide latitude in determining what can be purchased under such empowering statutes. The generalization may be made that in most jurisdictions a local school board's decision to purchase equipment will be sustained by the courts unless it can be shown that the item is far removed from the realm of desirable equipment for carrying on the purposes of a public school. This is particularly true if the material will be available for the use of all students within broadly defined categories. In several states through the years where courts have held that particular items could not be purchased under implied powers of local boards, corrective legislation has been passed so as to give local boards the power deemed necessary. There are, of course, limits beyond which local boards of education still may not go, however desirable an item may be.

Occasionally a parent or a taxpayer objects to some material used for instructional purposes in the schools. When local authorities permit the use, legal recourse may be had to the courts on allegation that the discretion of the local board of education has been abused or that constitutional rights are being infringed by the teaching. In most instances, the issue can be resolved by permitting the children of the aggrieved parent not to participate in the instruction which is offensive. In order for a court to require the removal of a publication completely from the curriculum, it would have to be shown that the volume actually did teach doctrines of a sectarian nature or doctrines subversive of the government, would grossly offend the morals of the community, or was intended to promote bigoted and intolerant hatred against a particular group.

Chapter VII

DETERMINING TO WHOM IT IS TAUGHT

Compulsory Education Statutes

One of the keystones of education in the United States is the state compulsory education law. These statutes establish both the right to attend public school and the duty to do so or to obtain equivalent education elsewhere. Generally there is a range of ages during which a child must obtain instruction, and a range during which he may do so at his option.

PRIVATE SCHOOLS: Compulsory education laws, despite any wording found in the statutes, cannot require attendance at public schools. In 1925 the Supreme Court of the United States rendered the interpretation that it was a constitutional right of parents to send their children to privately operated schools instead of the public schools if they so desired. In the historic decision the Court invalidated an Oregon law which had required that children between certain ages attend public schools.

In its opinion, however, the Supreme Court indicated that the state had the power to establish reasonable standards covering non-public schools. The states vary widely as regards degree of regulation of private schools. Some are rather strict, whereas others have almost no practical check on the quality of instruction in private schools.

HOME INSTRUCTION: Many of the compulsory education laws provide that children may receive "equivalent" education elsewhere than in school. Interpretation of the word "equivalent" is the basis of an increasing number of cases in recent years. Not only are the statutes in the various states unclear as to whether instruction at home satisfies the compulsory education requirements, but also in disagreement are the views of courts. Elements considered by some courts in determining whether home instruction is equivalent to that obtainable in a school include: level of education of the person teaching the child at home; qualifications in regard to teaching methods of the person doing the instructing; content of the instruction at home; teaching materials used; time spent by the child on education; educational proficiency of the child relative to his age and intelligence; and social development of the child.

ENFORCEMENT: Almost universally compulsory education laws are enforced on the local, as distinguished from the state, level. The parent or guardian who fails to have his child comply with such a statute is himself in violation of the law with a criminal penalty possible.

Ill-health normally is an excuse for not obeying compulsory education laws for the duration of the sickness. Also, if a child is mentally or physically handicapped, he cannot be compelled to attend instruction unless appropriate provisions are made for him. Statutes relating to education of the handicapped have become numerous since World War II.

Under certain circumstances irregular attendance may be considered a violation of a compulsory education law. It has been held that the need to work in order to earn money is not an excuse in and of itself. Neither in general is the contention that religious tenets are the reason the child attends irregularly. Thus, a Moslem child was required to attend school on Fridays despite the religious significance of that day to that faith. Furthermore, a parent cannot keep his child home because of disagreement with a school board regulation or because of objection to his child's assignment. The recourse of withdrawing one's child from public school as a protest is not legally open to a parent unless he provides equivalent instruction.

In most states compulsory education laws work in conjunction with child labor laws which regulate the employment of minors. Usually the authority to issue work permits to children within the compulsory education age bracket is vested in local school officials so that the child labor law and the compulsory education law can complement one another in the best interests of individual children and the state. Many laws stipulate that children of compulsory education age who are permitted to leave school to work must attend continuation classes which local school authorities must establish if there are a certain number of affected children in the school district.

Admission Requirements

HEALTH: It is within the power of the state to be certain that children attending public school are in reasonably good health so as not to infect others and so as to be able to profit from instruction. To this end the constitutionality of vaccination requirements is today well settled. Uniformly in the many cases on this point the courts have upheld the power of the state to enact such a requirement. The Supreme Court of the United States so ruled in 1922. There is, however, some uncertainty as to whether a local board of education can force a child to be vaccinated if there is no state statute on the matter. The cases here are divided, but where an epidemic threatened, local boards always have been deemed to have an implied power to require vaccination.

Even religious grounds are not justification for noncompliance with vaccination requirements. This is an illustration of where the courts have held the general welfare to be threatened by the exercise of a religious belief, and in such circumstances the general welfare must prevail.

Local schools have been sustained in requiring that pupils either present a certificate as to general health from a licensed physician or submit to health inspection conducted by the school doctor. If a parent refuses to comply with this type of health rule, his child can be barred from the schools and the parent held in violation of the compulsory education law.

AGE: When statutes specify that children in certain age ranges may or must submit to instruction, questions arise as to the legality of "cut-off" dates to determine eligibility.

In New York, for example, children "from seven to sixteen" must attend public school or get equivalent instruction elsewhere. Those "over five and under twenty-one" are entitled to attend the public schools of the district where they reside. To implement this type of statute a local school board may adopt reasonable rules regarding the date by which the age must be reached for admission during a given semester or year. Furthermore, the date can be changed at the discretion of the board unless the matter is controlled specifically by statute or by regulation of state-level educational authorities. Generally local boards may admit children below the minimum age required by law, although they have no authority to raise the minimum age. The use of tests as a basis of admission for children under a specified age is not clear legally.

The factor of age in connection with grade assignments within a school is treated later in this chapter.

RESIDENCE: Whether a child has a right to attend school in a given school district depends upon where he has his legal residence. It is generally held that a child has the right to attend the schools of the district in which he is actually living. The only major exception is when he is living in that district solely for the pupose of attending the school there. A child who for reasons other than schooling is living in a boarding house generally is entitled to attend free the schools of the district containing the establishment. The same is true for a child living with a relative, even though the relative is not his legal guardian.

Where the father pays taxes is usually of no consequence. That is to say, if the father pays taxes in one district but the child is living in a second district, the fact that the father is not paying taxes to the district in which the child is going to school does not mean that the child is to be excluded from free public education there. On the other hand, normally a child is entitled to free schooling only in the district where he lives, not in another district where his father may happen to pay taxes. A child living in one district with his father who owns a business and pays taxes thereon in another district has been held ineligible to attend free the schools of the latter district.

If a parent desires his children not to attend the public school of the district of residence, he can send the child to a private school or, in some states, provide instruction at home. Also he may be able to make arrangements to send him to a public school in an adjoining district. This would normally require paying the tuition rate set by the district receiving the child. There is, however, no compulsion on a district to accept tuition pupils in the absence of a statute. A few states have laws requiring a school district to admit on a tuition basis pupils not living in the district provided the schools in the district are not thereby overcrowded. Several courts have ruled that, regardless of whether tuition is paid, express statutory authority is needed before a district is permitted to accept non-resident students.

FEES: Whether fees can be charged children in public schools is largely dependent upon the wording of the state constitution and pertinent statutes. In most states the situation is not clear. Generally the issue focuses on "incidental" fees or fees for special services. Tuition fees as such would be prohibited in virtually every jurisdiction. Some courts have flatly ruled out all fees. Others have sustained small fees under similar circumstances. The former courts interpret "free" public education literally. The latter courts hold that "free" applies to tuition only and does not preclude fees for "extras." As illustration, the teaching of subjects not offered in the curriculum to those whose parents are willing to pay for the service has been upheld in several cases. The educational program of the school must not be hampered if such an arrangement is to be approved judicially. Also, the fee must be for something the child cannot reasonably expect to be furnished at public expense. Obviously this last criterion is difficult to apply. For example, if a class trip is considered part of the regular curriculum, then a fee for it would not be acceptable; if the trip is not so considered, a fee would be permissible.

Assignment and Promotion Policies

The power to classify pupils and to determine academic standards lies within the discretion of school authorities.

It is primarily on the local level where most decisions are made by school board policy and profession implementation of administrators and teachers.

PLACE OF INSTRUCTION: Designation of the school building to which a child will be assigned is the prerogative of the school board. There is no inherent right of a child to attend the school nearest his home. A school board cannot, of course, make assignments on an arbitrary basis. It has the authority, however, to determine that a handicapped pupil can profit more from being placed in a separate school than in a regular school without proper facilities to care for his disability. This power has been sustained by courts over parental objections when there was sufficient evidence to support such a finding by the school board.

Assignments may not be based solely on a consideration of race where such consideration militates to the disadvantage of the minority group. Where it is necessary to take account of race in order to disestablish the dual school systems in those states which separated the races prior to the Supreme Court decision of 1954, race can be a factor in assignment. Indeed, it must be until the dual school system is converted to a unitary one. Further, as amplified in Chapter XV, there is no constitutional bar against states or local districts reassigning pupils to create better racial balance in schools in the interests of better education for all.

GRADES AND COURSES: The assignment of students to grades lies within the power of school authorities acting on reasonable bases. Initial assignment of students transferring from other school districts or from private schools can be based on an examination. It has been decided that no unlawful discrimination results from requiring for admission to high school an examination to be successfully passed by those who had previously studied outside the school system while not requiring the examination of those from within the system.

School authorities may set up academic prerequisites for assignment to particular courses. A child does not have the right (nor does his parent) to demand that he be allowed to enter every course he would like to sample. On the other hand, school officials must be able to justify prerequisites they establish.

Although a child of compulsory school age must be admitted on the basis of age alone, his assignment and his advancement through the grades may be based on factors other than age. Such factors could include training completed, knowledge possessed and innate ability. The awarding of diplomas is also subject to the preceding considerations. A child has the right, however, to receive a certified statement as to the time he has attended school and the work he has completed.

Parental Excuses

The right of parents to select, within limits, what their children shall learn is well recognized in the common law. Indeed the whole concept of compulsory education is a limitation on the complete right of parents in early England to educate their children as they saw fit.

If a parent does not wish his child to be taught sometime, the weight of judicial opinion is to the effect that the child can be required to submit to the instruction only if it is essential to good citizenship. Otherwise, the child must be excused. If the failure of a child to study a subject renders him unfit to pursue another study desired by the parent, school authorities cannot be forced to permit the child to enter the other study. But school authorities generally cannot punish a child for refusing to study a subject at his parent's direction unless that subject is required by statute. In that situation, the constitutionality of the statute comes into question, with the right of the state to require that children be educated as a basis for good citizenship to be weighed against the right of parents to control the upbringing of their children.

In the cases on this point the reasoning of the parents is an important element. Many cases that have reached the courts have been connected with religious views. Although religious belief is not necessary to assert a parent's right to make a reasonable selection of courses for his child, where religious bases are given the courts seem especially disposed to uphold the parent. Several courts have stated the additional stipulation that for parental excuses to be honored the rights of other children must not suffer.

Exclusions from School

Children who are mentally or physically unable to profit from instruction in the public schools can be excluded therefrom by local boards of education. The area of education of the handicapped is currently a subject of much legislative action, and duties and discretionary powers of school boards in relation to it are increasingly being defined in state statutes.

If a child is so handicapped that his presence interferes with the smooth operation of the school, courts have sustained his exclusion. This has been the general holding both in cases involving physical disability and those involving mental incapacitation.

Further it is not necessary to retain in school children who are so insubordinate as to disrupt the school. In such instances, police and welfare authorities often become involved.

The statutes and the courts recognize that to exclude a child from public school is a grave matter. The interests and welfare of the other students, however, are held to be paramount to those of an affected individual. Special schools for very abnormal children operated by local or state authorities other than the board of education are to be found in most jurisdictions.

Apparently becoming more widespread is the issue of married students wishing to continue in school. The question arises most frequently in connection with girls. The weight of judicial authority is that so long as the married pupil is within the age range entitling him to attend school that right cannot be denied merely on the basis of marriage. If the deportment of a married pupil is such as to render his presence in school undesirable, he can be dealt with on that basis. On the other hand, a majority of courts have held that a child who has married is no longer subject to the compulsory education law if he does not wish to continue school.

Chapter VIII

DETERMINING WHO TEACHES IT

Control of qualifications and working conditions of teachers is within the legal power of the state. Recent years have brought a trend toward increased state level regulation of staff personnel policies through statutes which require local boards to do certain things or which set up statewide minimum standards below which local boards may not go. There has also been an increase in the number of statutes granting local boards specific authority to act at their own option on items in the personnel area.

In all states except Hawaii local boards of education are the employing bodies for teachers and can employ anyone licensed to teach within the state. Legal conditions of employment for teachers, in addition to those imposed by state statute, are established by the employment contract with the local board of education. Teachers are considered by the law to be public employees rather than public officers.

The Teaching Certificate

Each of the fifty states has set up requirements which must be met before one may obtain a certificate or license to teach therein. The certificate in effect is an assurance to local boards of education and to the public that the possessor is qualified to teach.

There is substantial variation among the states in requirements for teaching certificates. The general prescriptions do not differ so markedly as do specifics. In some states many certification requirements are covered by statute. In others — and the trend is in this direction — certification standards are made the prerogative of the state educational agency (state board, chief state school officer, and state department).

Points covered in requirements for teaching licenses generally include number of years of college level study, areas of study in college, and general items such as health, citizenship, and age. Some states require certain specific courses on rather narrow subject matter. Most states issue a variety of licenses covering various areas of specialized work in the public schools.

The power to grant a certificate is construed by many courts as implying the power to revoke it for cause. Revocation of a certificate, however, is a very severe penalty as it can deprive one of his livelihood, and, therefore, good cause must be shown. Revocation of certificates in many states is governed by statutes which set forth specific causes. Generally it has been held that an enumeration of causes is considered exhaustive, and a certificate cannot be withdrawn for a reason not included in the list.

Local Employment Practices

It has been stated that only certificated teachers are eligible to teach in the public schools. Many questions have gone to courts, however, regarding the time at which the teacher must possess a certificate in order to enter into a valid contract with a local board of education. Many statutes are vague and simply use the expression "time of employment." In some states this has been held to mean that it is necessary for the teacher to possess the certificate at the time the contract is signed, whereas in other states the meaning is that the teacher must possess a certificate before actually beginning to teach.

A non-certificated teacher cannot be paid, according to the courts, even if he has been allowed to teach. The law considers a teacher who teaches without a certificate to be merely a volunteer and not eligible for payment from public funds. Indeed many statutes provide criminal penalties for board of education members who pay non-certificated teachers.

Local boards of education are empowered to require qualifications beyond the minima prescribed by the state. This discretion, however, can be limited by the state. Local boards can stipulate, as examples, more academic training, passing of an examination, and a certificate of health. They cannot, however, apply religious or political qualifications for teaching. Neither can they discriminate among applicants on the basis of race. Board rules prohibiting the employment of married women teachers have been sustained in several states in the absence of statutes barring the practice.

In initial employment the burden of fitness is legally upon the candidate; the board of education can exercise its discretion in any manner not forbidden by law. By statute certain items may be removed from the realm of consideration by boards. Examples include age and sex. Also, in recent years the courts have established the principle that, merely because a board has discretion in deciding whom it will employ, it does not have the power not to employ for an unconstitutional reason. Examples include race, religion, and membership or non-membership in a labor union.

Duties of Teachers

There is considerable confusion, in both teaching and legal circles, as to the duties of a teacher under his contract. It is clear that a teacher may be assigned to teach any subject for which he holds a certificate. Duties may encompass any aspect of that subject. It has been held, for example, that a teacher in physical education may be required to coach football or basketball.

Problems arise when teachers are asked to render services other than those involved in classroom instruction or in activities directly related thereto. A California appellate court sustained the right of a local board of education to require an English and social studies teacher to supervise a proportionate share of school athletic events. The court reasoned that it was within the scope of the teacher's contract to supervise students to protect their welfare at events conducted under the name and auspices of the school provided that such responsibilities were reasonable in number and hours and that such duties were distributed impartially among the staff. On the other hand, a Pennsylvania court has ruled that taking tickets at an athletic contest on a Saturday was beyond the scope of employment of a teacher.

A New York court has given some examples of things that could or could not be required. "Any teacher may be expected to take over a study hall . . . and to devote part of his day to student meetings . . . . Teachers in the field of English and social studies and undoubtedly in other areas may be expected to coach plays . . . . Teachers may be assigned to supervise educational trips which are properly part of the school curriculum." On the other hand, according to the court, a teacher may not be required "to perform janitor service, police service (traffic duty), school bus driving, etc. . . . [or] a duty foreign to the field of instruction for which he is licensed or employed."

Freedom of Teachers

Teachers are bound to observe the state and local curricular requirements and prohibitions treated in Chapters V and VI. Beyond these, however, and within general limits of propriety, they are free to teach as they see fit.

They cannot use the classroom to advocate personal or political beliefs. Thus, the urging of pupils to have their parents vote for a particular candidate has been judicially deemed improper. Courts also have sustained dismissals of teachers who in class have made derogatory remarks about the government or individuals in office. Immoral statements and actions are further grounds for disciplinary proceedings against teachers.

Activities of teachers outside the classroom are subject to reasonable regulation associated with the welfare of the school. It is generally agreed that there are some types of conduct in which teachers might engage outside the classroom which would render them unfit to serve as examples to children in school. Just where the critical point is, however, is as indefinite in the eyes of the courts as it is in the eyes of citizens in general.

The courts generally have upheld the rights of teachers to exercise the normal prerogatives of citizenship. Teachers are not barred from signing petitions and actively campaigning for candidates of their choice on their own time. In most jurisdictions teachers are not required to resign their positions in order to become candidates for, or serve in, political posts. Of course, if the duties of a political officer should conflict with those of teacher, adjustments must be worked out.

Gradually won over the years has been the right of teachers to belong to organizations which have some stated political purposes deemed by many not to be consistent with the best interests of the government. This issue has been a persistent one through the years, with periods of concentration at particular times of international tension, the greatest occurring following World War II. Loyalty statutes requiring that teachers disavow membership in certain organizations or participation in certain activities proliferated.

In 1952, however, the Supreme Court found that the due process clause prohibited a state from attempting to bar disloyal individuals from its employ by excluding them "solely on the basis of organizational membership, regardless of their knowledge concerning the organizations to which they had belonged." The Court emphasized that "membership may be innocent" and that "a state servant may have joined a proscribed organization unaware of its activities and purposes." It held that "indiscriminate classification of innocent with knowing activity must fall as an assertion of arbitrary power."

Again in 1961 the United States Supreme Court found a provision in an oath repugnant to the Constitution. In this instance the Court did not declare the entire oath invalid, but merely knocked out a provision on the ground of unconstitutional vagueness. The issue to be decided, in the words of the Court, was "whether a State can constitutionally compel those in its service to swear that they have never 'knowingly lent their aid, support, advice, counsel, or influence to the Communist Party.'" The unanimous Court emphasized that the "provision is completely lacking in . . . terms susceptible of objective measurement." On similar grounds in 1964 by a seven-to-two vote the Court struck down another loyalty oath requirement for teachers.

In 1966 the Court in a five-to-four decision added the stipulation that for a teacher to be barred not only did it have to be shown that he knowingly belonged to an organization advocating violent overthrow of the government, but that he personally had participated in activities designed to this end or that he joined the organization with specific intent to carry out its illegitimate purposes. This new criterion led many state courts to invalidate loyalty provisions for teachers in those states, especially after the Supreme Court reaffirmed its stand during each of its next two terms and increased the five-to-four margin to six-to-three when one justice was replaced.

In 1967 the Court in effect reversed its 1952 position relative to a series of statutes in New York designed to keep subversive personnel from the schools. During the intervening fifteen years, many rules and regulations had been added to supplement the statutes, leading to what the majority in 1967 considered a "regulatory maze" with wording of prohibitory rules lacking precision of meaning. However, in its opinion the Court restated the general principle that a state did have the power to protect its educational system from subversion. Subsequently the Supreme Court upheld the requiring of loyalty oaths providing that the signer would support the federal and state constitutions and faithfully execute his duties.

The early 1950's produced a wave of legislative investigations of alleged subversive activities, many of these investigations focusing on the schools. One case to reach the United States Supreme Court involved a professor of a city college in New York City who was summarily dismissed for refusing to answer questions relating to Communist Party activities asked by a legislative investigating committee. There was a provision in the New York City Charter requiring termination of services if an employee refused to reply to questions regarding "the property, government, or affairs of the city . . .

on the ground that his answer would tend to incriminate him." The provision originally had been placed in the Charter to deal with matters related to misuse of public funds, but was here applied in a teacher loyalty case.

By a five-to-four margin the Supreme Court in 1956 ruled invalid the dismissal of the teacher without a trial. The majority said, "At the outset we must condemn the practice of imputing a sinister meaning to the exercise of a person's constitutional right under the Fifth Amendment. . . .Since no inference of guilt was possible from the claim [of the Fifth Amendment] before the federal committee, the discharge falls of its own weight as wholly without support. There has not been the 'protection of the individual from arbitrary action' . . . the very essence of due process."

Added, however, as the last paragraph was the following:

"This is not to say that . . .[the teacher] has a constitutional right to be an associate professor of German at Brooklyn College. The State has broad powers in the selection and discharge of its employees, and it may be that proper inquiry would show . . . [the teacher's] continued employment to be inconsistent with a real interest in the State. But there has been no such inquiry here. We hold that the summary dismissal of appellant violates due process of law."

Two years later came another five-to-four decision holding that if a teacher is questioned by the superintendent of schools about his activities in the Communist Party and he refuses to answer, he can be dismissed. The majority agreed with the Pennsylvania Supreme Court that the statutory ground of "incompetency" covered a teacher's "deliberate and insubordinate refusal to answer the questions of his administrative superior in a vitally important matter pertaining to his fitness." The majority thought the questions asked by the superintendent were relevant to the issue of fitness and suitability to serve as a teacher. They found "no requirement in the Federal Constitution that a teacher's classroom conduct be the sole basis for determining his fitness." The Court differentiated this case from the previous one by stating that a public employer has the right to ask questions relevant to matters which could affect an employee's efficiency and that an employee has the duty to answer such questions when they are put by his employer.

The right of a teacher publicly to criticize school authorities was considered in 1968 for the first time by the Supreme Court. A teacher wrote a letter to a newspaper criticizing the manner in which the board and superintendent had handled proposals to raise new revenue and the way in which revenues were allocated, especially between sports and academic subjects. The letter contained no implication of dishonesty. The Court held in favor of the teacher and stated that unless teachers were allowed to speak out freely on questions of public educational policy, a knowledgeable segment of society would be eliminated from the public discussion. The Court noted that no question either of maintaining discipline by immediate superiors or harmony among coworkers was present. Even though there were some errors of fact in the teacher's letter, the Court found that they were not intentionally placed there and that the teacher had not recklessly made false statements. Furthermore, there was no evidence that the teacher's performance of classroom duties had been interfered with, nor that the general operation of the schools had been seriously adversely affected.

Dismissal of Teachers

Generally speaking there are three legal statuses of employment for teachers: term contract, continuing contract, and tenure. In the term contract situation, employment after the expiration date is dependent upon a new contract being offered by the board of education. If this is not forthcoming, the teacher has no legal redress. He simply is not being reemployed. Some states have provided for continuing contracts which remain in effect for the following year unless the teacher is specifically notified several months in advance of termination at the end of a year. Such a provision gives a teacher the opportunity to look for a new job during the period that there are openings. The section "Local Employment Practices" earlier in this chapter applies in situations where contracts are not renewed.

Almost three-fourths of the states on a state-wide basis, or for all but the very small districts, have tenure statutes which prescribe the procedure which must be followed before a teacher may be dismissed. Some other states have such statutes covering only the very large districts. Although tenure laws differ in detail, all have certain elements: a teacher must be given timely notice that his dismissal is contemplated; he must be given a statement of specific charges which are being made against him; he must be afforded the right to a fair hearing at which time he has an opportunity to refute the charges or to show that they do not warrant dismissal. Many of the statutes also specify a definite procedure for appeal. Such appeal may be initially to state educational authorities or directly to the courts. The appeal may be a review of the hearing or a new trial on the facts.

Chapter IX

CONTROLLING PUPIL CONDUCT

The legal aspects of controlling pupil conduct can be broken into two broad categories. The first grouping pertains to rules, and the second to punishments for violations of the rules. This area is one in which there is a vast body of common law which must be considered in conjunction with any codified law. General principles are easily stated, but applications in specific situations are elusive. On the highest level of generalization, it may be said that local school authorities have the power to make reasonable rules governing pupils designed for effective school management and may punish pupils for violations of such rules in a reasonable manner. Reasonable punishment would involve not only the punishment itself, but the procedure for determining it.

Rules and Regulations

IN GENERAL: In a specific state there will be some items of pupil personnel administration which are governed by statute. So long as the statute is constitutional, local school authorities must act in accordance with it. Where there is no statute, however, or where the statute is vague, the common law prevails. Most of the rules and regulations governing student conduct are established on the local level. Some are set up in the form of local board of education policy. Others are established by the superintendent, the principal, or the classroom teacher. Rules must be designed to achieve proper ends, and they must be reasonable in terms of these ends. The burden of proof in cases challenging the validity of a regulation is on the complaining party, the legal presumption being that the rule is valid. It should be noted, however, that in recent times the courts are examining in greater detail the bases for rules governing student conduct.

School authorities clearly have the power to establish rules governing student behavior. Thus, such conduct as talking in class, leaving the classroom without permission, fighting, disobeying instructions, and annoying other pupils can be prohibited. It is not necessary that the rules be written in cases of generally unacceptable conduct. Obviously every act which interferes with the orderly operation of the school cannot be anticipated by teachers or administrators and specifically forbidden by a written rule. They are empowered, however, to control any disruptive behavior when it becomes evident. How far they can go in preventing a form of behavior in anticipation of a disruption is not clear in the abstract.

It must be emphasized that school authorities cannot prohibit behavior of which they disapprove on that ground alone. The barred conduct must interfere with the orderly operation of the school or with the rights of other students.

The Supreme Court considered its first case of student conduct unrelated to religious conviction in 1969 when it held that school authorities in Des Moines, Iowa, could not bar the wearing of black armbands by students to voice disapproval of United States participation in the Vietnam conflict. Wearing of the armbands had been prohibited because school officials thought it would lead to a disturbance. There was none, and the Court found that the authorities had cut off a form of constitutionally protected political expression. In the case there were several significant facts. There was not a uniform ban on all political symbols, but specifically on black armbands. The students that wore the armbands made no attempt to encourage other students to wear them, and were definitely not wearing them to defy school officials. The Court specifically pointed out that at issue was a matter of political expression—a significant First Amendment right which all citizens, including students, have. The Court was not satisfied under the facts that school officials had a sufficient basis for invading that First Amendment right.

DRESS AND APPEARANCE: In recent years the courts have considered many cases dealing with regulation of student dress and appearance. In different fact situations courts have reached different conclusions regarding the power of the board of education to regulate such matters as style of hair and length of skirt. Different weights have been given by different judges in different circumstances to such points as the rationale for the rule in question, the clarity of the statement of the rule, the circumstances in which the rule was challenged, the evidence of need for the rule, and the circumstances surrounding the violation of the rule.

It is clear that school boards may ban kinds of dress detrimental to proper discipline or morals in the school. Thus, the wearing by boys of jackets symbolizing defiance of proper school authority, or by girls of tight-fitting sweaters or slacks could probably be prohibited even though a general ban on such items would likely be impermissible. Also, for safety, an item like a long-haired, inflammable sweater could be prohibited near stoves in a home economics class. On the other hand, it is well settled that schools may not require pupils to wear particular items of clothing. An exception would be gymnasium garb which could be required for certain activities on a basis of safety of pupil or damage to facilities.

SECRET SOCIETIES: A frequently litigated area is that of control of fraternities and sororities by educational authorities. The weight of judicial opinion is clearly to the effect that local school authorities may forbid students to join secret societies operating within the school system. It has generally been held that membership in such societies by students may be prohibited regardless of the desires of the parents in the matter. Also courts find immaterial whether the society has members outside the school population and whether it meets after school hours. An attempt to control membership in fraternities during the summer vacation, however, has been ruled to be beyond the school board's power. Justification for the legal sanctioning of rules barring membership in fraternities and sororities is that thereby the interests of the student body as a whole are better served because such membership tends to interfere with the purposes and discipline of the school. Despite the fact that the Supreme Court of the United States ruled in 1915 that there is no federal constitutional question involved in a restriction on secret societies, the matter has reappeared in courts rather steadily through the years. Similar judgments, however, have been forthcoming.

CONDUCT OFF SCHOOL GROUNDS: The line between the authority of the school and the authority of the parent in relation to control of pupil conduct off school grounds is frequently hazy. Also, of course, the police may be involved in some instances.

The authority of the school over pupils definitely extends beyond the school grounds under some circumstances. The criterion as to whether a rule of conduct may be enforced by school personnel is the nature of the conduct in relation to the school program, not the place of the conduct. Thus, school authorities have been sustained by courts in punishing pupils for acts committed away from the school.

Behavior on the way to and from school can be controlled to a considerable extent. Examples of court approved rules include those which forbid such acts when on the way to or from school as using profanity, molesting other children, and fighting. Also, it may be required that pupils go straight home unless parents direct otherwise.

Even after pupils reach home, or on holidays, school authorities can regulate conduct prejudicial to the efficiency of the school or the related well-being of other students. As mentioned previously, membership in secret societies can be forbidden even if activities are carried on off school grounds (except during the summer vacation period). Members of an athletic team representing or purporting to represent the school are not free from school control because games are played after hours and off school premises. Disorderly conduct by students which brings the school into disrepute can be controlled by punishing offenders. Thus, public drunkenness, disrespect for teachers after school, and written statements defaming school personnel are out-of-school offenses punishable by school authorities.

Punishments

IN GENERAL: It immediately becomes apparent that a reasonable rule can be enforced in an unreasonable or illegal manner. Several generalizations about punishments which legally may be inflicted emerge from the scores of cases on the point.

First of all, the punishment must "fit the crime." That is to say, the gravity of the penalty must be reasonably related to the gravity of the offense. Also any penalty must be given for a legitimate purpose, such as, maintaining discipline, generally promoting the welfare of the school or helping the pupil in his own interest to correct a fault. Where school authorities are properly motivated, the courts have gone far in sustaining their common law right to administer reasonable punishment. The school authorities are said "to stand in the place of parents" when the children are committed to their care during the school day. Actually school personnel cannot go so far under the law as can parents, and even powers of parents to punish are not unlimited.

In the case of punishments, as was true in the case of rules, reasonableness cannot be decided in the abstract. Some punishments might be reasonable in some situations and not in others. For example, detention after school is a judicially approved method of punishment in almost all circumstances. There are some situations, however, where it probably would not be approved by courts. Thus, if through detention after school a child should miss the school bus and, therefore, be subjected to the hazards of the highway on the way home, or if the parent instructed the child to return home immediately after school, detention might be held unreasonable. Similarly the withholding of privileges as a punishment is judicially condoned. However, the line between activities that are withdrawable privileges and those that are rights of all pupils under the law is not clear in some cases.

Legally there always exists a presumption that school authorities have acted correctly in administering any type of punishment. It is further presumed that the authorities have acted in good faith. Evidence to the contrary, of course, can refute these presumptions. The burden of proof, however, is on the person bringing the action against school authorities in punishment cases.

SUSPENSION AND EXPULSION: The most serious punishments open to school authorities are suspension and expulsion. Suspension implies a temporary exclusion from school pending the correction of some defect. Expulsion is of a more permanent nature, perhaps for a year or more. Conditions for expulsion normally are set forth in state statutes, and in most jurisdictions a pupil can be expelled only by official action of the board of education. Older cases have held that it is not necessary for the pupil or parent to be heard before a child may be expelled. The more modern view, however, seems to be that in cases of expulsion the right to be heard must be observed. Because the expulsion of a child from school involves his statutory right to attend school—a very valuable legal right—the courts examine carefully the reasons for expulsion. Uniformly, however, they recognize that the right of a child to attend school is conditioned upon his submission to appropriate rules of conduct and upon his presence not being detrimental to the health, morals, or educational progress of other pupils.

CORPORAL PUNISHMENT: The most frequently litigated punishment is "corporal punishment." It should be noted that corporal punishment would be any touching of the body with intent to correct a child's behavior. The courts through the years have upheld the infliction of corporal punishment which is reasonable in manner and moderate in degree. Such is firmly rooted in judicial precedent. A few states have statutes specifically pertaining to corporal punishment. These often indicate ways in which the punishment is to be administered. For example, in Montana it is to be administered only in the presence of the principal. Pennsylvania has a statute which makes explicit the common law right of teachers "to exercise the same authority as to conduct and behavior over the pupils . . . as the parents" while pupils are at school or between home and school. A New Jersey statute is unusual in that it forbids the use of corporal punishment in the schools of that state except under specified circumstances. Many local boards of education have regulations on the matter.

In determining whether an instance of corporal punishment is legally permissible, courts consider such variables as the nature of the offense, the instrument used to administer the punishment, any permanent injuries derived from the punishment, motivation of the teacher, and physical characteristics of the child punished. The last category would include age, sex, size, and physical condition of the child. Thus, an instance of corporal punishment permissible in the case of a fifteen year old might not be for a six year old, and a penalty reasonable for a boy might not be for a girl of the same age.

It should be noted that three distinct types of legal action can grow out of corporal punishment cases. One is a criminal action for assault and battery brought by the state against the teacher. The end sought is a penalty against the teacher, such as a fine or imprisonment. The second legal action is a civil one for assault and battery brought against the teacher by parents of the child. The object of the parent's suit is to obtain damages (financial redress) from the teacher. The third type of possible action is a proceeding against the teacher by the school board charging that the particular instance of corporal punishment constitutes incompetency and therefore ground for dismissal. The three types of legal consequences of corporal punishment are separate and are not necessarily interrelated.

ACADEMIC PUNISHMENT: Occasionally an academic punishment is given for a behavioral offense. Thus, a child's grade in a course is lowered or his diploma is withheld on a basis other than lack of proficiency in the subject or in the academic requirements for graduation. The generalization is clearly to the effect that academic punishments are not to be meted out for disciplinary infractions unless these infractions are such as to render the student clearly unworthy of the academic benefits or unless such a punishment is sanctioned by statute. Even where diplomas are legally withheld, students must be given statements covering the work they have completed.

Chapter X

BEARING RESPONSIBILITY
FOR PUPIL INJURIES

Accidents are common among all human beings, but especially so with children. Most injuries are the fault of the injured and not due to the negligence of other parties. There are many situations, however, where harm can be attributed to acts or failures to act of others. The law requires that in such cases the person who caused the injury must make reimbursement. Payments of this nature are known as "damages." The term "liability" means financial responsibility.

In regard to accidents to pupils while under the care of the school, three legal parties may be involved as defendants: the school district (or school board as an entity), school board members as individuals, and employed personnel.

Liability of the School District

Under the common law governmental agencies are not responsible for damages caused by their negligence or by the negligence of their employees. Thus, in the absence of a statute to the contrary, it is the general rule that one cannot recover damages from the school district for injuries suffered due to the negligence of the school district in providing unsafe conditions or in hiring personnel who acted negligently.

The situation is in marked contrast with the law governing private employers and employees. There the law holds employers responsible for the damages to third parties caused by an employee in the discharge of his duties. Through the years two basic reasons have been given by courts for this doctrine of governmental immunity. The first is essentially one deriving from the theory that "the king can do no wrong."

The government is deemed unable to commit wrongs for which its citizens have redress without its giving express permission for that redress. The other basic reason is a more practical one—the availability of funds with which to pay judgments for damages. The taxpayers would have to bear the brunt of judgments since the only funds available to public bodies are tax funds. The thought has been expressed by many courts that budgets of school districts would be undermined by the uncertain element of damages and the quality of the educational program might suffer great harm if funds were diverted to pay damages. This line of reasoning leads to the conclusion that the individual's interest in being reimbursed for injuries suffered through the negligence of the school district must yield to the greater interest of the public at large in the effective operation of the schools.

The social injustices caused by this situation and the advent of insurance have caused some legislatures and courts to re-examine the doctrine of governmental immunity as applied to school districts in the light of the present era. Since the doctrine is derived from the common law, it can be modified either by statute or by judicial interpretation.

Some state legislatures have made school boards liable for negligence to the same extent that private corporations are liable. A few statutes specify a maximum amount of recovery, and in several states the limit of recovery is the amount of insurance carried by the district. Statutes cover negligence of employees in the line of duty, as well as unsafe conditions on premises brought about by negligence of the school board. In a few of the states where school districts as such are immune from liability for negligence, statutes make the districts liable for payment of damages assessed by a court against an employee of the district for injuries to a third party arising out of the employee's negligence when acting within the scope of his employment.

As school districts engage in more activities, the question arises whether some of the functions are actually governmental in nature, as distinguished from proprietary. School districts in some states have been held by courts not to be covered by governmental immunity when engaged in proprietary functions. In general a proprietary function is one which the local government unit is not required to perform and which is often carried on by private enterprise or is used as a means of raising revenue. Examples of district immunity failing to cover an activity because it was judicially considered proprietary are found in Arizona where a school stadium was rented for a football game between teams from two other school districts, and in Pennsylvania where a school district operated a summer swimming program open to all comers upon payment of a fee. It should be noted that although monetary considerations enter into the classification of a function as proprietary, the mere charging of a fee does not make an activity proprietary rather than governmental.

Liability of School Board Members

It is relatively rare that a school board member is held individually liable for negligence. Partly this is due to the fact that most acts of school board members are not the direct causes of injuries. Furthermore, because the school board has power to act only as a corporate unit, the actions of board members as individuals are limited. Also, under the common law public officers are not responsible for damages resulting from mere mistakes in judgment when they have acted with good intentions. If such were not the situation, it would be very difficult to get people to accept public office, particularly an unpaid office such as that of school board member.

Nevertheless, if a board member does not act honestly and in good faith, he is not protected from responsibility for his actions. Thus the common law did not protect from liability school board members who employed a relative of a board member as bus driver over the protests of citizens who claimed the bus driver to be reckless and incompetent. The death of a child killed when this man was driving the bus was held to be attributable to the act of employment by the board members, deliberately done without justifiable cause.

School board members in other instances have been held personally liable when they failed to follow specific statutory procedures with resultant injuries. When the law requires a board to follow a particular procedure, all discretion is removed from the board. It if can be shown that the board members have either with gross negligence or with intent deviated from statutory procedure, they may be held personally liable for consequences. For example, board members were held individually liable for damages following a bus accident because they had failed to see that buses were insured as expressly required by statute.

Liability of Teachers

IN GENERAL: An individual teacher or other employee of a board of education is subject to the same law covering liability for negligence as are citizens in general. That is to say, a legal action could be maintained against a teacher for injuries to a pupil resulting from the negligence of the teacher. Except in those few states having statutes making school boards responsible for payments of judgments against teachers, the teacher himself would have to pay the judgment. Since most teachers are not financially favored, certain practicalities regarding collection of judgments must be considered along with purely legal concerns.

In a few states liability insurance taken by school boards might cover teacher employees. Also in some jurisdictions teachers have banded together to obtain group liability insurance. Of course, it is possible for an individual to get insurance covering his own liability. Attention should be drawn to the fact, however, that insurance really does not affect the question of liability; rather it provides for paying judgments up to an amount specified in the policy after liability has been established.

IN SPECIFIC SITUATIONS: When the child is under the care of school authorities, the law requires that these authorities act in a reasonably prudent manner under the circumstances. The standard of care varies with the maturity of the child and the nature of the activity in which the child is engaged. Professional personnel are held legally to a standard of care commensurate with their professional training. Doing something that a reasonably prudent teacher would not have done or failing to do something that a reasonably prudent teacher would have done under given circumstances with resultant injury to a pupil can form the basis of a negligence suit.

It should be emphasized that neither the teacher nor the school board is the insurer of the child's safety. Unavoidable accidents to children far exceed those caused by someone's negligence. On the other hand, injuries do occur sometimes because professional personnel have not acted properly. A key element is often that of foreseeability or anticipation of consequences. If a reasonably careful teacher could foresee a possible harmful outcome and did not act to prevent it, he would be negligent. Hence, in connection with the use of equipment, the teacher must be certain that the equipment is not faulty through inspections at regular intervals. Moreover, the teacher must not authorize the use of dangerous equipment without specifically instructing the children as to the proper use of the equipment and warning them of the dangers in misuse. The actual use of dangerous equipment should be supervised by a teacher, and special care should be taken to prevent the unauthorized use of such equipment.

There should be supervision for all aspects of activity during the time that the child is on the school grounds. This would include recess periods and lunch periods. The supervision must be adequate in terms of the number of supervisors on duty. The proper number would vary in terms of the activity and the age of the children. Those supervising an activity should be competent to carry on the supervision. The placing of younger children under the care of older children as monitors in some situations might not be justifiable from a legal point of view. In other circumstances, however, it might be perfectly proper. Another element regarding legal adequacy of supervision is the action of the supervisor. There could be enough supervisors and they could be competent, but if they do not act as reasonably capable teachers would, liability may result.

It cannot be overemphasized that the responsibility of school personnel is that of acting reasonably carefully to protect pupils from accidents and injuries. It is almost always possible to figure how an accident might have been prevented after it has occurred. Whether the teacher could have prevented the injury is not the test. The test is whether the teacher should have anticipated the injury and should have acted before harm was done.

For a teacher to be liable for injuries to a pupil, the latter must not have contributed to his own injury. Generally, for example, a teacher is not liable for an injury resulting from a pupil's deliberate disobedience of a rule. Nor does liability derive for injuries resulting from normal risks of an activity engaged in voluntarily by a pupil. An illustration is found in the sport of football. A student whose parents permit him to participate in football is considered to have voluntarily assumed the normal risks of the sport. The dangers assumed are those generally associated with the sport. Injuries resulting from the coach's negligence are still legally actionable.

Where an injury has occurred, it is the responsibility of school authorities to render first aid, that is, the minimum necessary under the circumstances until trained medical assistance can be obtained. To fail to render first aid might leave school authorities liable. However, to go beyond first aid in the treatment of an injury can also result in liability.

The courts in cases of alleged negligence take into account the fact that persons operating under emergency conditions, such as when an accident has happened, cannot be expected to act as effectively as they would under normal circumstances.

It is well to reassert that negligence constitutes a question of fact to be determined in each individual case. The standard of legally acceptable conduct is that of the teacher of average prudence, not the overly cautious or clairvoyant.

Chapter XI

MANAGING SCHOOL PROPERTY

Acquisition

In most states local school boards are specifically empowered by statute to acquire property and to construct buildings necessary for the public schools. Even in the absence of such express statutory authority the courts uniformly have upheld as an implied power the right of school boards to buy property.

This should not be taken to mean that boards have unlimited power to purchase property for school purposes. The courts have gone quite far, however, in finding in favor of school boards when it could reasonably be shown that the property was needed for school development. A major exception is to be found where a school board bought some land for a farm, contending that the purpose was covered by implication in a statute requiring teaching the principles of agriculture. The court ruled otherwise.

Purchases of land for playgrounds and for building stadiums for athletic contests have been upheld. The land in such instances does not have to be contiguous to school-owned property. The courts are not in agreement, however, as to whether general board powers are sufficient to permit the construction of living quarters for teachers.

Financial aspects of acquiring property are discussed in Chapter XIII.

In most jurisdictions school boards can acquire land by eminent domain where it is impossible to purchase it. Private property can be taken over for public use by schools provided that fair compensation is made to the private owners and that the land is really needed for a school purpose. Often procedural points related to eminent domain are set out by statute.

Most courts have found that a school board has the authority to rent property needed for school purposes in situations where the board reasonably might decide that rental was the only way, or the best way, to acquire certain school facilities. For example, while new school buildings are being built, renting facilities often appears to offer the only means by which schools could feasibly be conducted in many situations. Statutes in some states put limitations on the authority to rent. Hence, some facilities might not be acceptable for renting under statutes regarding safety requirements for school rooms. Also, it has been held that facilities may not be rented in a parochial school building in which symbols of the religious domination are maintained in view.

Generally where authority to insure is not expressly granted by statute, courts have sustained the contention that the right of a school board to acquire and hold property gives it an implied power to insure that property against fire and disaster. There is some question, however, as to whether a school board can insure property in a so-called "mutual association," in which type of insurance plan there is no set premium, payments depending on needs of the association to pay out money for losses. Some courts have held that in such an arrangement the school district might suffer heavy losses and, further, that such insurance would constitute the lending of the credit of the school district to benefit private individuals.

Maintenance and repair of buildings in most jurisdictions are responsibilities of the local board of education. In some areas, however, statutes give this function to the municipality with the same boundaries as the school district.

Use

IN GENERAL: With the notable exception of California, the uses to which a school building can be put are left to the determination of the local board of education. The Civic Center Act in California requires local boards to grant free use of school facilities to "parent-teachers associations, Campfire girls, Boy Scout troops, farmers' organizations, clubs, and associations formed for recreational, educational, political, economic, artistic, or moral activities." It is not uncommon for a state to require that school facilities be used as polling places or that they not be used for religious purposes or for subversive purposes. Beyond such prescriptions, however, most states do not have legislation pertaining to required or permissible uses of school facilities.

Therefore, if a particular type of use of a school building is not approved by the local board of education, in the absence of a state statute, there is no legal action in general to force the board to allow the use. On the other hand, there are many judicial decisions relative to the legality of certain uses of school buildings permitted by local boards where objections were raised.

Most cases on this topic are brought by taxpayers who object to school expenditures for the maintenance and operation of buildings which are used for non-school purposes, who allege that a specific use of school buildings is barred by legal provisions for the separation of church and state, who object to use of the buildings by particular groups, or who claim that their businesses are being hurt by some use of school buildings.

When all of the cases are considered, there emerges considerable conflict as to the specific non-school uses that can be made of school facilities. There is discernible, however, an increasing tendency of the courts through the years to liberalize the use of school facilities if local school boards so decide. There is, of course, no authority vested in a local board to allow school property to be used for purposes which would interfere with the school program. Courts in many states have recognized this overarching stipulation. Nor is a board of education authorized to permit uses of the school building which would result in damage to the building which must be repaired by money raised through taxes.

CHARGES FOR: In many jurisdictions school boards charge fees for the use of school buildings to cover expenses of light, heat, and custodial services. In the absence of a statute prohibiting it, it would seem that school boards have authority to charge such fees. The courts, however, are divided as to the authority of school boards to charge an amount which could be considered a rental payment, as distinguished from a fee covering incidentals. It appears definite that school boards cannot provide special facilities to be used primarily for purposes of rental to community groups. In scores of cases courts have stated that school boards are not set up to engage in commercial enterprises. Some courts, though, have sustained school boards in renting facilities which were not needed for school purposes at a given time. When renting has been judicially approved, the courts uniformly insist that there be no interference with the school program and no damage to the building.

Another factor considered by courts when legal action is brought to halt a non-school use of buildings is whether the property is used for an event where there is an admission charge. Where the proceeds were devoted to school purposes, such as providing school equipment or making possible a school-connected activity, some courts have permitted such activities. Also, a few courts have not barred incidental private gain so long as the primary purpose of an event was essentially in the public interest.

BY RELIGIOUS GROUPS: Many cases have arisen regarding the use of school buildings by religious groups. The rule seems to be that it is the use to which the building is put that is the decisive criterion, not the identity of the user. Thus, if a religious group wishes to sponsor some activity for the benefit of the community as a whole, a school building might legally be used. If, on the other hand, a religious service were to be conducted, the school property probably could not be so used. In the latter circumstance, an additional element sometimes considered is whether the church group would be using the building over a short or a long period of time. Several decisions sustain the temporary use for religous purposes of such facilities.

There seems to be no question that a local school board may prevent a school facility from being used by any group with religious affiliations for any purpose. The board, however, may not discriminate or differentiate among religious groups. If one religious group is permitted the use of the school building for a particular purpose, then all religous groups must be given the same opportunities.

BY OTHER GROUPS: The last statement applies equally to groups of any nature. If one organization in a category is permitted to hold a meeting of a certain type, similar groups must be given the same privilege. School boards may not discriminate against organizations because board members or some taxpayers are hostile to the opinions or program of the associations. A legal exception is made if an organization has unlawful aims. In some jurisdictions it has been held that if a local board generally permits political uses of its facilities, it cannot bar a specific group unless there is sufficient evidence that the group is truly "subversive." But boards have been upheld in denying a use where it could be shown that a clear and present danger existed that public disorder and possible damage to the school building would result from the proposed use.

In recent years, however, the courts have been looking more thoroughly into the reasons offered by school boards for denying use of school buildings to specific groups or persons. For example, when a nationally known folk singer critical of the war in Vietnam was prevented from giving one of a series of concerts by reputable musicians in a school auditorium, the court invalidated the school board's denial, which had been defended on the ground the performer was a controversial figure.

CONFLICTING WITH BUSINESS: Cases involving uses of school property which allegedly conflict with private interests are frequent. The courts are agreed that school facilities cannot be used primarily for personal gain. Such is not permissible even if substantial rentals are charged by a school board. If commercial gain is merely an incident to a completely legitimate use of school facilities, however, generally such use would be judicially permitted.

The operation of a school cafeteria, for example, does indeed interfere with the business of some commercial establishments. Yet, the courts uniformly have sustained the legality of the operation of a cafeteria so long as it is handled on a non-profit basis and is not deliberately designed to take customers from private restaurants. Two other key considerations related to operation of a school cafeteria are whether the enterprise is considered part of the curriculum and whether it is restricted to students and staff. It has been held, however, that an occasional parent's eating in the cafeteria does not change its basic nature.

Schools which sell supplies to students at cost probably are acting within the law if the operation is non-profit with any proceeds going directly into a school fund. A few courts, however, have prohibited such activity, indicating that it is beyond the power of the local school board even though the motivation for the activity is laudable.

Disposal

All buildings and other property used for public school purposes within a school district are in legal contemplation the property of the state, rather than of the local district. This is true even though the property has been financed entirely from funds raised by bonds or taxes on the local level. The legal rationale is found in the fact that school districts are agencies of the state. They hold property in trust for the sole purpose of providing educational facilities.

Thus, the legislature may determine not only how property is to be used, but also how it is to be disposed of. Disposal of school property is usually covered by statute. The courts have been reluctant to give local school boards as much discretion in disposing of school property as they have in its acquisition. Statutes must be carefully observed in detail.

School boards are not permitted to sell for a nominal fee, or to donate, school property unless the transaction is permitted by statute. Thus, a school board which intended to sell an unneeded building to a church group for a sum less than could have been obtained from another purchaser was prevented from so doing by court action.

Chapter XII

PROVIDING TRANSPORTATION

In General

In 1900 there was virtually no legislation pertaining to school transportation. As this aspect of school operation has burgeoned, so has legislation pertaining thereto, with the result that today each state has rather detailed prescriptions. These statutes cover such points as who has the right to be transported, who may be transported at local school board discretion, safety standards for buses, colors and markings for identification of buses, requirements for school bus drivers, operating regulations for school buses, and liability insurance. Many states make special provisions for transportation of handicapped children.

Some state agencies other than those set up for educational purposes usually are assigned some responsibilities related to school transportation. Licenses for school bus drivers generally are issued by the regular state licensing agency. The motor vehicle bureau is responsible for inspection and the reporting of traffic accidents involving school buses. State traffic codes normally contain penalties for passing school buses.

Minimum requirements for bus drivers are established on the state-level in most states. About half of the states have regulations pertaining to the character of school bus drivers. Slightly fewer have stipulations regarding the physical condition. About twenty states require the school bus driver to hold a special license. Every state has a minimum age requirement for school bus drivers and a few states specify maximum age. A recent trend is toward a requirement that school bus drivers have some knowledge of first aid.

Local school boards can furnish transportation in one of three general ways: with buses owned and operated by the school district; with buses contracted from private operators; and by reimbursement to parents for providing transportation for their children. In many cities the common carriers transport school children at reduced fares in accordance with franchise provisions.

Generally a school district can purchase its own buses and operate them if transportation is required or is optional with the local school board. In some states there is special legislation authorizing local districts to issue short term bonds, to make short term loans, or to levy special taxes for the purchase of buses. In other states the purchase of buses is to be included within annual current expenditures. Some states have special state financial aid for purchasing school buses. Where statutes do not include the amount that parents are to receive if they transport their own children, parents may be paid any reasonable amount by the local school board.

In nine out of ten states transportation statutes are linked to state financial assistance to local districts for transportation. The power of the state to pay from state funds for all or part of the cost of pupil transportation apparently is well settled. Frequently litigated issues involve whether a local board can furnish transportation for distances shorter than the state requirements at local expense, whether boards must furnish transportation to some pupils under certain conditions regardless of source of funds, and whether local boards can transport certain classes of pupils regardless of source of funds.

Criteria of Eligibility

PURPOSE: The attitude of courts through the years has been not to consider the provision of transportation as an implied power of local boards of education. This situation probably gave impetus to the enactment of many of the aforementioned kinds of statutes. Also, generally speaking, the courts have been much less liberal in interpreting transportation statutes than they have been in construing other statutory powers of local boards of education.

Statutes providing for the transportation of children "to and from school" frequently have been held not to permit local boards to spend money for transportation of children to other school-connected activities, such as field trips and athletic contests.

Yet, the constitutionality both of mandatory and permissive state legislation relating to purposes for which pupils must or may be transported has been upheld by courts except in a few instances involving conflict with state constitutions on the matter of transporting pupils to private or sectarian schools. With this one exception it appears that most state legislatures are unrestricted in requiring or permitting school children to be transported at public expense and in establishing stipulations covering the operation.

In those instances where transportation laws are mandatory local boards are left no discretion and must furnish the transportation regardless of cost involved. The fact that a separate bus route had to be established to pick up one child living in a particular area was held not to excuse a local board from complying with the state law. Moreover, a lack of funds does not justify the failure to provide transportation except in those states where certain elements of the transportation statutes are subject to local action by the voters.

DISTANCE: Almost all of the states have transportation legislation treating distances from school in terms of rights and privileges of school children and duties and options of local boards of education. Frequently the distance lived from the school in order for high school students to be eligible for transportation is greater than that for elementary school pupils. Many statutes are mandatory in regard to pupils who live beyond a certain distance from school and permissive for other pupils. Some state statutes do not specify a fixed number of miles, but use rather vague terms like "residence remote from the school."

Generally speaking, maximum distances that children can be transported at public expense are not provided, although a few states have such provisions pertaining to children attending non-public schools. Where a local district is permitted the option of furnishing more transportation than is required by state law, the basis of classification of pupils eligible for transportation must be clear, and the program must be uniformly administered.

The courts do, of course, take into account the fact that it takes a reasonable amount of time to establish transportation facilities within a school district. Furnishing of transportation to some children within a certain category and not to others during a limited period of time when instituting a program has been held justifiable. Otherwise, all children in a certain classification as to distance from home to school must be treated uniformly. The one possible exception involves road hazards which are discussed in the next section.

Distance from a child's home to the school is judicially considered to be via the shortest public route. Furthermore, transportation does not have to be on a door-to-door basis. A child can be expected to meet the school bus at a distance from his home which is within the limits of the statute.

TRAFFIC HAZARDS: Whether a school board can utilize the element of traffic hazards as a criterion in addition to distance in determining which children should be transported is not clear in many states. Administrative rulings on the state level in several states bar the practice unless a distance factor is considered concurrently. In other words, in these states if any child living one mile from school is transported because of dangerous road conditions, then all children living one mile must be carried regardless of the absence of hazards on their routes to school.

Some courts have not followed this line of reasoning and have indicated that consideration of road hazards by local boards is proper in establishing transportation policies. Of course, the determination as to what constitutes a road hazard of sufficient danger to warrant transportation must be made on a reasonable basis. The basic issue revolves around the implied powers of local boards of education. It seems clear that by statute the legislature could prohibit, permit, or require that road conditions be considered in the provision of transportation.

Children in Non-Public Schools

One of the major social policy issues in the United States is the question of whether transportation should be furnished at public expense to children attending non-public schools. All four possible legal situations exist among the fifty states. In some states the expenditure of public funds for this purpose is prohibited by explicit constitutional or statutory provision or by court interpretation. In others it is expressly required by state law. A third category comprises those states where statutes specifically make the matter one to be handled on the basis of local option. In the fourth classification are states where there is no statement in the written law on the point and the courts have not ruled on it.

In 1947 by a five-to-four majority the Supreme Court of the United States found no federal constitutional bar to the furnishing of transportation to children in non-public schools on the same basis as to children in public schools. The majority reasoned that in such a circumstance it was the child who was receiving the aid, rather than the school. The aid was considered to be in the category of a welfare benefit which could be extended to all children if the state so desired. But it must be emphasized that this Supreme Court decision answered basically only one legal question: Does the *federal Constitution* bar use of public funds for transportation of children to non-public schools? The negative answer leaves the matter to the individual states. The states have not followed a common path, as is amplified in Chapter XIV

Liability

The transportation of pupils is one of the most hazardous activities engaged in by school boards today. Thus, the question of liability for accidents is a pertinent one. As pointed out in Chapter X, in most states school districts as such are not liable for their negligence or that of their employees. If, for example, a bus is poorly maintained and the inadequate maintenance results in injury to a student, or if negligence of a driver results in injury to a student, no recovery from the school district is generally possible unless specifically provided for by statute. About half of the states require that liability insurance be carried on school buses that are publicly owned. In most others the power to acquire liability insurance is expressly granted to local boards. Where legislation requires or authorizes a school district to purchase liability insurance covering bus operation, the immunity of the district is not waived by taking out insurance. These statutes usually provide that recovery of damages resulting from negligence may be had only up to the limit of the insurance carried.

Over half of the states have provisions which require private owners of school buses to carry liability insurance. In other states it would seem to be clearly within the power of the local board of education to refuse to let a contract for bus transportation to a company which did not carry adequate insurance. In Kentucky, a state requiring insurance for private operators, school board members have been held personally liable for damages when this provision was not observed by the board.

The courts expect school bus drivers to exercise a degree of care above that required of drivers of ordinary private automobiles. School buses must be stopped only in spots where students may alight safely, and they must not be started again until children are on the sidewalk. Bus drivers are responsible for exercising care that children are not injured in going from the bus to the sidewalk; they are not, however, legally expected to insure the absolute safety of the children.

Rules and regulations governing the conduct of students on school buses can be enforced by drivers.

Chapter XIII

PAYING FOR SCHOOLS

Federal Funds

The amount of money expended by the federal government for public education is not very significant. This level of government at present pays only approximately eight percent of public school costs for the country as a whole, the figure having hovered around four percent prior to the Elementary and Secondary Education Act of 1965.

Federal funds for public school education are devoted primarily to assisting states and local districts in supporting specific projects. Major examples of activities aided by federal funds include vocational education (since 1917), school lunches (since 1946), programs in mathematics, science, foreign languages, and guidance (since 1958), and programs associated with improvement of schooling for educationally deprived children (since 1965). Some financial assistance is provided to local school districts where enrollments have been greatly increased by influxes of families of servicemen or civilian workers connected with governmental defense projects.

The question of federal financial aid to public school education has been a persistent one in Congress, especially since World War I. The complex issues which in combination have prevented any federal aid for general purposes or substantial aid for special purposes are beyond the scope of this volume. Political, rather than legal, considerations have dominated, although many of the controversial points have important legal ramifications.

There seems to be little question that the federal government is empowered under the "welfare clause" of the Constitution to make appropriations for public school education. The purposes and administrative arrangements for the funding are basically problems of policy, rather than of law. The situation is amplified in Chapter II.

State Funds

LEGAL BASE: As repeatedly emphasized in the preceding chapters, public education is legally a function of the states. How a state chooses to finance its public schools is a decision of the legislature. There is extremely wide variation among the states both as to percent of cost borne by the state and as to how state-level funds are distributed to local units. For the United States as a whole, about forty percent of the revenue for public schools comes from the state level. The range (excluding Hawaii) is from under ten percent in Nebraska to over seventy percent in Delaware.

It is well established through a long series of judicial decisions that the state has the power to tax all the residents of the state and to use the money where it is needed within the state so long as some rational basis for distribution exists. Furthermore, the state can distribute the money to different classifications of districts in different manners so long as the basis of classification is reasonable and so long as all districts within a classification are treated similarly.

RATIONALE FOR PROVIDING: In the early days of the nation funds raised locally were only slightly supplemented by the state. Through the years, however, the state share has been increasing. The increase in state-level funds has been due to several factors, some essentially theoretical and some essentially practical. In the first category is a complex of reasons grounded in the legal concept of education as a state function. It is argued that the state has a definite responsibility for seeing that adequate education is provided for *all* of its children regardless of where they happen to live within the state. Legally local school districts are creations of the state and their boundaries are subject to alteration by the state. In every state there is substantial variation in wealth among local school districts. Some of the poor districts and some of the wealthy frequently have boundaries which are currently indefensible on any rational basis. The state, in theory, must assume the obligation of equalizing to a degree the educational opportunities afforded children of the state. This can be done without upsetting long-established civic and political traditions by furnishing money to help local districts, especially the less economically favored, to provide adequate educational programs.

An important practical consideration is the fact that the state is in a far better position to obtain funds than is the local government unit. The sales tax is the greatest source of revenue on the state level. Other taxes with high yield on the state level are income and gasoline levies. These taxes are impractical on the local level except in very large cities, primarily because they would defeat their purpose of raising money by tending to drive customers and businesses out of town and because their effective and economical administration is difficult on a small base. This aspect of the finance problem relating to tax administration is further discussed subsequently under "Local Funds."

METHODS OF DISTRIBUTION: There are many variations in the methods by which state-level funds are allocated to local school districts. The traditional basis of state aid distribution is by some sort of flat grant plan. A flat grant is an appropriation based on an easily determined objective measurement unrelated to financial ability of a district or to local finance practices, such as, number of pupils, number of teachers, or number of classrooms. In several states constitutional provisions require that certain funds be prorated on a specified flat grant basis. There is, however, a trend away from this sort of distribution.

A variation of the flat grant is the matching grant, whereby the state supplies a certain amount of money if the local district allocates a specified sum. The ratio between state and local funds is determined by the legislature. Matching funds are used frequently to stimulate local-level progress in areas which are not well developed parts of the educational program. Examples would be library facilities, psychological services, and testing programs.

The trend in state-level financing of schools is toward distributing state money so as to approach financial equalization of educational opportunity within the state. Such a system involves the use of state funds to supplement local funds in equalizing educational opportunity in a state to the extent that every child is assured a minimum educational program in terms of dollars spent on him, with equal tax effort on the part of all citizens of the state. This minimum program is generally called the "foundation program." The elements included in the program when costs are calculated vary among the states using the plan. "Equal effort" in theory means that each citizen is allocating the same percent of his economic resources to pay for the program. Essentially the plan involves three elements.

First, a figure is set to be the minimum expenditure for the education of each child in the public schools of the state. Second, a figure is set for minimum local effort in terms of tax rate for school purposes on *full* value of property. Third, state funds are then allocated to each district to increase the amount of money raised locally by the minimum tax to the amount needed to carry on the minimum program. Local districts which wish to provide a quality of education above the state minimum may add local funds beyond those required by the equalization formula with no decrease being made in money received from the state.

A relatively new basis for distribution of state funds involves what is known as "shared costs." This plan combines features of both matching and equalization. A ratio between state and local funds is established for each local district. The ratio depends upon the financial ability of the district: the less wealth per pupil, the higher the proportion of expenditures reimbursed by the state. A maximum figure may be placed on local expenditures which will be supplemented on the ratio basis, but the ratio would apply up to that figure regardless of additional expenditures of local funds.

The funds distributed by any of the aforementioned methods could be designated by the state for use by local districts for specific purposes, or the use could be left entirely to local determination. It is not necessary that all state funds be allocated by the same method. Combinations are common. Some states establish minimum educational requirements which must be met before state funds are forthcoming, such as length of school year and qualifications of teachers.

Local Funds

OBTAINING OPERATING FUNDS: The marked variation among the states as to ratio of funds from state and local sources has been pointed out. In two-thirds of the states local funds support more than 50 percent of the school budget. About 95 percent of all local school funds are derived from the property tax. Obviously this is a tremendous burden on a single tax, especially on one that has become less effective as American society has been changing so that ownership of real estate is not the valid measure of wealth that it was in the earlier days. Also, it should be noted that the property tax has to sustain the financing of other governmental functions performed on the local level, such as, police, fire, health, and recreation.

Furthermore, local governmental units, whether they be municipalities or school districts, have only those taxing powers which specifically are granted them by the state. Thus, even were it possible for a local community to devise additional taxes which might help support local-level functions, such taxes cannot be levied without approval of the state. Most states have been reluctant to give local units special taxing powers. Some problems related to finding effective taxes to be administered on the local level were pointed out earlier in this chapter.

Certain communities in some states find themselves unable to raise more money for support of education because of state-imposed limitations on the local property tax rate. From a legal point of view this matter is squarely within the power of the state to remedy.

Despite the problems related to the property tax as virtually the sole source of local funds for government operation, much can be done in many locations to improve the administration of the tax. In many communities reassessments have not been made to reflect recent changes, particularly increases, in property values. Tax assessors generally are appointed on the local level, and some assessors are not sufficiently skilled for their posts. In many localities there are substantial amounts of tax exempt property, some now used for purposes which might no longer warrant tax exemption. Many authorities believe that the various bases for tax exemption of property should be re-examined. The privilege is an indirect subsidy to those having it, and municipal and school governments are prevented thereby from obtaining additional funds from the property tax.

SPENDING OPERATING FUNDS: Although details differ—often even among districts within a state—approval of the local school budget for current expenditures is effected in one of three basic manners.

The method that removes expenditures for public schools farthest from the control of the voters is to place final authority somewhere in the municipal government, usually in the city council. This puts public education in a financial situation directly competitive with local government functions insofar as claims on tax resources are concerned. It has been pointed out previously, however, that the state has the power to require that certain priorities be afforded education under this structure.

A second method of final budget approval is the vesting of the authority in the local board of education. In such jurisdictions the school board adopts the budget and either levies, or causes to be levied by another agency, taxes to meet the budgetary requirements. Since board members in these areas are popularly elected for the sole purpose of operating the school system, control of spending is somewhat closer to the people than in the first method. (In general, appointed boards may not levy taxes.)

The third method involves submission of a proposed budget directly to the electorate for approval. In some districts the voters must accept or reject the budget as a whole, or possibly in two or three large categories. Other statutes provide for school district meetings where voters discuss the budget and can directly increase, decrease, or approve as submitted specific items in the budget. Voter approval may be restricted to certain budget items. There is a trend away from direct voter approval of budgets.

FUNDS FOR BUILDINGS: New buildings are financed in a manner different from that discussed above for current expenditures. The usual method of obtaining money for purchase of sites and construction of facilities is by the school district's borrowing through the use of bond issues. The amount borrowed, plus interest, is paid off gradually over a period of years.

The funds raised through bonds must be used only for the purposes specifically set forth in the bond issue. This principle is rigorously enforced by the courts. The question of whether a specific item is encompassed by the purpose of the bonds frequently must be judicially resolved.

Authority to issue school district bonds is entirely dependent on the statutes, and these must be scrupulously followed. Many states have constitutional or statutory prescriptions setting maximum limits on bonded indebtedness for a municipality, or a school district, or the two units combined where they have the same geographic boundaries. Generally a bond issue must be approved by the qualified voters in a special election held for that purpose.

Chapter XIV

CHURCH-STATE RELATIONS
AND EDUCATION

Since 1947 the Supreme Court of the United States has rendered six "First Amendment" decisions covering seven specific aspects of church-state relationships in public education. In addition, the Court has declined to review many other cases decided by state or federal courts on this subject. Treated have been both the use of public funds in connection with schools operated by sectarian groups and the place of religion in the curriculum of public education.

Transportation to Non-Public Schools

The first of these Supreme Court cases was decided in 1947. It involved a local board of education in New Jersey which had authorized reimbursement to parents of expenditures by them for the transportation of their children to parochial schools on the same basis that reimbursement was provided to parents of children attending public schools. (The school district did not run its own school buses.) A taxpayer filed suit challenging the procedure on two grounds: expenditures for the benefit of any non-public school children would violate the due process clause of the Fourteenth Amendment in that all people were taxed to help some carry out a private purpose, and taxes were used to help support and maintain church-operated schools contrary to the prohibition of the First Amendment (made applicable to the states by the Fourteenth).

The decision of the United States Supreme Court was by a five-to-four margin. All nine judges seemed to agree that the due process clause of the Fourteenth Amendment was not violated in that a state legislature *could* find the funishing of transportation to non-public school children in general to serve a public purpose.

It was on the contention that the contested regulation constituted a "law respecting the establishment of religion" where the Court sharply divided. It should be noted that the division of the Court was actually on the application of a principle, rather than on the principle itself. The majority opinion upholding the procedure included the following clear-cut statement:

"The 'establishment of religion' clause of the First Amendment means at least this: Neither a state nor the Federal Government can set up a church. Neither can pass laws which aid one religion, aid all religions, or prefer one religion over another. Neither can force nor influence a person to go to or to remain away from church against his will or force him to profess a belief or disbelief in any religion. No person can be punished for entertaining or professing religious beliefs or disbeliefs, for church attendance or non-attendance. No tax in any amount, large or small, can be levied to support any religious activities or institutions, whatever they may be called, or whatever form they may adopt to teach or practice religion."

The Court said that it had decided in 1925 that parents can discharge their duty under state compulsory education laws by sending their children to a religious school rather than to a public one "if the school meets with secular educational requirements which the state has power to impose." Challenged in that case had been an Oregon statute requiring that all normal children between certain ages attend public schools. There was strong evidence that enforcement of the regulation would put private schools, both sectarian and non-sectarian, out of business. It was ruled that the state's power did not extend so far as to infringe property rights of those engaged in a business not contrary to the public welfare. Technically, the legal issue was not a church-state one. A private non-sectarian school was a plaintiff, as was a sectarian school. The Court's opinion did not mention the First Amendment. The case was decided on the basis of the Fourteenth Amendment's prohibition against depriving persons of property without due process of law. The Court took the occasion, however, to discuss rights of parents in the upbringing of their children, and stated that they had the right not to send their children to public school if the school they preferred met reasonable state requirements. The state's interest in the education of the young was held subordinate to that of parents *provided* the substituted education met minimum requirements. There was no mention whatsoever of using public funds in any way in relation to those attending private schools.

In the New Jersey bus case it was held that the regulation "does no more than provide a general program to help parents get their children, regardless of their religion, safely and expeditiously to and from accredited [private] schools." Thus it was reasoned that the "benefit" was to the child, not the church-school. The majority opinion closed with the following statement:

"The First Amendment has erected a wall between church and state. That wall must be kept high and impregnable. We could not approve the slightest breach. New Jersey has not breached it here."

The four dissenters, in applying the principle of the "wall of separation," found the distinction between aid to the pupil and aid to the church school to be an invalid one. They thought that the cost of transportation was as much a part of the total expense as the cost of other items in the education process and thus was indeed a financial aid to sectarian schools.

It must be emphasized that this decision of the Supreme Court places the matter in the hands of the individual states—to be decided through their constitutions, legislatures, and courts. The Supreme Court merely found that there was no federal Constitutional bar. It did not find any federal Constiuional right to such transportation.

Individual states have continued to differ since this decision. Some require local school boards to furnish the transportation, some permit local school boards to do it at their discretion, and some forbid local school boards to do it. Not only do statutes vary, but court interpretations of general state constitutional provisions regarding church-state separation are not consistent. Statutes providing for transportation of children to church-related schools were challenged on state constitutional grounds in nine states during the decade 1960-1969. Courts invalidated the statutes in Alaska, Delaware, Hawaii, Oklahoma, and Wisconsin. No church-state violation was found in Connecticut, Michigan, Ohio, and Pennsylvania. In no other areas, except perhaps race relations (see Chapter XV), have the opinions of judges differed more in regard to similar constitutional and statutory wording.

Textbooks for Students in Non-Public Schools

The greatest impetus to the so-called "child benefit" theory came in 1968 when the Supreme Court by a six-to-three margin upheld a New York statute requiring that textbooks be furnished for the use of children attending non-public schools. In 1930 the Supreme Court had found no federal Constitution bar to furnishing the *same* textbooks to children in private schools that were used by children in public schools. The highest court in that case accepted the reasoning of the Supreme Court of Louisiana to the effect that the child, not the school, benefited. It bears emphasis, however, that the case was not presented to the United States Supreme Court as a church-state case, but as a use-of-taxes-for-a-private-purpose case. The First Amendment issue was ignored.

The New York legislative extension was that the books for private school children were to be "approved by" a board of education. Also, read literally, the statute provides that if any public school board in the state approves the use of a particular book, it must be made available to any child in the state requesting it for use in a non-public school. The majority of the Supreme Court based its reasoning on that used in the New Jersey bus case. But the writer of the majority opinion upholding bus transportation, Justice Black, dissented and stated that the majority in 1968 was misreading the opinion he wrote for the Court in 1947. Oddly, the distinction between "the same books" and "books to be approved by a school board" was completely ignored by the majority of the Court. The opinion emphasized, however, that no "religious books" were to be furnished, and that "the record contains no suggestion that religious books have been loaned." The Court took judicial notice of the fact that "religious schools pursue two goals, religious instruction and secular education." Further, the Court found that the statute met the test of constitutionality enunciated in its 1963 opinion in the Bible-reading-Lord's-Prayer case (discussed subsequently): "a secular legislative purpose and a primary effect that neither advances nor inhibits religion."

"Released Time" for Religious Instruction

In 1948 the Supreme Court in an eight-to-one decision found invalid as a violation of the First Amendment a plan in an Illinois school district whereby religious teachers, employed at no expense to the public school but teaching within the school buildings and subject to the approval and supervision of the superintendent of schools, instructed children on a voluntary basis. The two key points in the decision were that school buildings were used and that "students who did not choose to take the religious instruction were not released from public school duties; they were required to leave their classrooms and to go to some other place in the school building for pursuit of their secular studies . . . [and] students who were released from secular study for the religious instructions were required to be present at the religious classes." This procedure was found to be "beyond all question a utilization of the tax-established and tax-supported public school system to aid religious groups to spread their faith." The Court then expressly restated the quotation from its opinion in the New Jersey bus case to the effect that aid to *all* religions was unconstitutional whether done by the federal or state government.

In 1952, however, by a six-to-three margin the Supreme Court upheld a New York plan whereby children on written request of their parents could be excused for one hour a week to attend sectarian religious instruction off the school premises. Even though the children who did not partake of this instruction were required to remain in school, the majority of the Court decided that the arrangement was not an "aid" to religion, but rather an "accommodation" of religion. The majority found that there was no coercion and that the school authorities were "neutral," doing "no more than release students whose parents so request." (The question as to whether "coercion" was present was one that was vigorously challenged in the dissents.) The majority maintained that they were following the Illinois case, but that they could not extend it to invalidate the released time program "unless separation of Church and State means that public institutions can make no adjustments of their schedules to accommodate the religious needs of the people."

Prayers and Bible Reading

A decade passed before another question in this area was accepted by the Supreme Court. In 1962, with only one dissent, the Court found that the following prayer could not be recited in the public schools as part of opening exercises, even though pupils who objected could be excused:

"Almighty God, we acknowledge our dependence upon Thee, and we beg Thy blessings upon us, our parents, our teachers and our country."

The prayer had been composed by the New York State Board of Regents and was recommended for use to local boards, one of which was challenged in the suit.

Without reciting any prior cases the Court discussed the history of the First Amendment and found a violation of the establishment clause. The Court emphasized that violations of the establishment clause do not depend upon a showing of direct governmental compulsion (as is necessary with the free exercise clause). The majority felt "it is neither sacrilegious nor anti-religious to say that each separate government in this country should stay out of the business of writing or sanctioning official prayers and leave that purely religious function to the people themselves and to those the people choose to look to for religious guidance." The Court further pointed out that what was barred was a "religious exercise," not use of "references to the Deity" on "patriotic or ceremonial occasions."

The following year the Supreme Court consolidated a Pennsylvania case and a Maryland case relative to Bible reading and the recitation of the Lord's Prayer as part of opening exercises in public schools. This 1963 opinion, unlike the 1962 one, contained extensive documentation showing that in invalidating both these religious exercises as part of the school program the Court was not deviating from its established precedents in the area of church-state-education relationships. Again, there was only one dissent.

After reviewing the many cases, the Court succinctly stated the crux of the matter as follows:

"The test may be stated as follows: what are the purpose and the primary effect of the enactment. If either is the advancement or inhibition of religion then the enactment exceeds the scope of legislative power as circumscribed by the Constitution. That is to say that to withstand the strictures of the Establishment Clause there must be a secular legislative purpose and a primary effect that neither advances nor inhibits religion. . . . The Free Exercise Clause, likewise considered many times here, withdraws from legislative power, state and federal, the exertion of any restraint on the free exercise of religion. Its purpose is to secure religious liberty in the individual by prohibiting any invasions thereof by civil authority . . . .

"The place of religion in our society is an exalted one, achieved through a long tradition of reliance on the home, the church and the inviolable citadel of the individual heart and mind. . . . In the relationship between man and religion, the State is firmly committed to a position of neutrality."

The Prospects

In 1968, on the same day that it released its decision in the New York textbook case, the Supreme Court modified one of its rulings which had been in effect for forty-five years. In 1923 the Court had held that one did not have standing to sue to halt an expenditure of the federal government based on his status as a taxpayer who was claiming that his taxes were being unconstitutionally expended. The lack of the right of taxpayers to challenge federal expenditures in the courts has reduced the extent of judicial scrutiny of federal expenditures. This is particularly true as regards church-state relations in the area of education.

Federal funds have long been used in connection with private education for purposes for which state funds in many states could not be used. The amounts of money and uses thereof have markedly increased since enactment of the many-faceted Elementary and Secondary Education Act of 1965. The 1968 procedural ruling (issued in a case where the substantive issue was federal funding in relation to church schools) grants taxpayers the right to sue to stop federal expenditures allegedly in violation of constitutional provisions which restrict the Congressional taxing and spending power. The establishment clause of the First Amendment is one such restraint on Congress.

Strong indications point to much litigation in the next few years in relation to uses of federal, as well as state, funds in connection with church-related schools. And there is no reason to anticipate a decline in the flow of cases related to the place of religion in the education afforded by public schools.

Chapter XV

RACE RELATIONS AND EDUCATION

In no important area of public policy have the Justices of the Supreme Court of the United States been so unified in their views as in cases relating to racial segregation in public education. The holding in each case decided by the Court since the initial one in 1954 has been unanimously rendered.

The Desegregation Decisions of 1954-5

It was not until 1954 that the Supreme Court of the United States had squarely presented to it the question, in the words of the Court itself: "Does segregation of children in public schools solely on the basis of race, even though the physical facilities and other 'tangible' factors may be equal, deprive the children of the minority group of equal educational opportunities?" The affirmative answer came when similar cases from five different jurisdictions (Delaware, District of Columbia, Kansas, South Carolina, and Virginia) were merged and treated in the now famous "Brown" decision. The Court concluded that "in the field of public education the doctrine of 'separate but equal' has no place. Separate educational facilities are inherently unequal. Therefore, we hold that the plaintiffs and others similarly situated for whom the actions have been brought are, by reason of the segregation complained of, deprived of the equal protection of the laws guaranteed by the Fourteenth Amendment." Having unanimously made this momentous promulgation in 1954, the Court said that "because of the wide applicability of this decision, and because of the great variety of local conditions, the formulation of decrees in these cases presents problems of considerable complexity. . . . We have now announced that such segregation is a denial of the equal protection of the laws. In order that we may have the full assistance of the parties in formulating decrees, the cases will be restored to the docket, and the parties are requested to present further argument [on several specific questions]...."

One year later, then, in 1955, the unanimous Supreme Court stated the following:

"Full implementation of these constitutional principles may require solution of varied local school problems. School authorities have the primary responsibility for elucidating, assessing, and solving these problems; courts will have to consider whether the action of school authorities constitutes good faith implementation of the governing constitutional principles. Because of their proximity to local conditions and the possible need for further hearings, the courts which originally heard these cases can best perform this judicial appraisal. Accordingly, we believe it appropriate to remand the cases to those courts. . . . The courts will require that the defendants make a prompt and reasonable start toward full compliance with our May 17, 1954, ruling. Once such a start has been made, the courts may find that additional time is necessary to carry out the ruling in an effective manner. The burden rests upon the defendants to establish that such time is necessary in the public interest and is consistent with good faith compliance at the earliest practicable date. To that end, the courts may consider problems related to administration, arising from the physical condition of the school plant, the school transportation system, personnel, revision of school districts and attendance areas into compact units to achieve a system of determining admission to the public schools on a nonracial basis, and revision of local laws and regulations which may be necessary in solving the foregoing problems. They will also consider the adequacy of any plans the defendants may propose to meet these problems and to effectuate a transition to a racially nondiscriminatory school system."

The First Decade Thereafter

Hundreds of cases in the following decade were decided by courts in the states which were forced to cease operating racially segregated school systems. Legislative and administrative plans of almost infinite variety were devised. "Good faith" and "all deliberate speed" were interpreted primarily by federal District Courts and federal Courts of Appeals. Except for the desegregation crisis in Little Rock, Arkansas, involving a state's challenge of a federal court order in 1958, the Supreme Court ruled on no public school segregation case until 1963, when it reversed the acceptance by lower courts of a Tennessee plan. Under that plan attendance areas would have been rezoned without reference to race, but a student would have been permitted to transfer from a school where he would be in the racial minority back to his former school where his race would be in the majority. The unanimous Court found that "it is readily apparent that the transfer system proposed lends itself to perpetuation of segregation." In 1964 the Supreme Court ordered that Negro children in Prince Edward County, Virginia, "get the kind of education that is given in the State's public schools." In this situation the public schools of the county had been closed to avoid desegregation, but white children were being educated in a system of private schools, which, through various stratagems, were being financed to a substantial extent out of public funds.

The Period beginning in 1965

As time passed the Supreme Court showed growing impatience with the failure of most Southern school districts to comply with the spirit of the desegregation decisions. In 1965 it took the step of ordering immediate relief for Negro students in an Arkansas district who, because of the grade-a-year desegregation plan adopted in 1957, were still in an all-Negro high school. Furthermore, the high school did not have as extensive a curriculum as that in the white high school. Also in 1965, the Court ruled that desegregation of faculties was necessary. In 1969 it approved the establishment by a lower court of a ratio of white-to-Negro teachers for each school in an Alabama district to serve as a guide for desegregation of staff there.

Three decisions delivered by the Supreme Court in 1968 treated the adequacy of the desegregation plans locally adopted. The question before the Court, in its words, was "whether, under all the circumstances here, respondent School Board's adoption of a 'freedom-of-choice' plan which allows a pupil to choose his own public school constitutes adequate compliance with the Board's responsibility 'to achieve a system of determining admission to the public schools on a non-racial basis [the stipulation set in 1955].' " The Court flatly stated, "The burden on a school board today is to come forward with a plan that promises realistically to work, and promises realistically to work *now*." Found unacceptable by the Court were freedom-of-choice plans which had not led to effective desegregation. The Court expressly did not rule out freedom-of-choice plans as a possible legal means for desegregation; it held that each plan must be examined in terms of its results, and that if other ways are reasonably available and promise speedier and more effective conversion to a unitary, non-racial school system, freedom-of-choice must be replaced. (See Addendum on page 111).

Trends in the South

Although variations in facts, as well as variations in attitudes of judges, make all-encompassing generalizations impossible, a few significant trends (accelerated markedly, if belatedly, in the late 1960's) can be noted. First, the courts no longer are accepting as readily excuses offered by local school boards for failing to make effective progress in desegregating. The courts are looking more closely at results rather than at intentions. Also to a greater extent they are ordering boards to take specific steps, rather than giving general directions. More burden is being placed on school boards, and less on parents and pupils, in the effectuation of desegregation. It is now firmly established that boards have an affirmative duty to disestablish the vestiges of the former dual school system, rather than simply to cease certain prior practices. More attention is being given to aspects of desegregation other than assignment of pupils. Desegregation of teaching staffs is a particular focus. The involvement of the executive branch of the federal government, both the Department of Justice and the Department of Health, Education and Welfare, has increased. The guidelines for desegregation promulgated by the Office of Education in 1965 have been very influential. So has legal aid for asserting Negro rights from the Department of Justice after the Civil Rights Act of 1964.

"De Facto" Segregation

Recent years have seen increased legal, as well as political, attention to what has become popularly known as "de facto" segregation. The term is applied to situations where individual schools contain large proportions of Negro students and where no action of the board of education or other government unit required or encouraged the development of that status. In general, housing patterns and applications of the "neighborhood school" policy of pupil assignment have been the causes of de facto segregation. It is to be recognized that in some districts in states which had no statutory or constitutional segregation prior to 1954, school board actions over the years contributed directly to the establishment of some of the racially imbalanced schools. Gerrymandering of school attendance zones, inconsistent application of transfer policies, and other discriminatory practices have existed in places in the North and West. Such situations constitute segregation by governmental act, and are covered by the Supreme Court decisions discussed previously. They are not de facto instances. It is where the racial imbalances have grown adventitiously that de facto segregation exists, and a different legal problem arises.

Emerging legal patterns in the area of de facto segregation are somewhat hazy due to complicated facts in specific cases and also to political and other non-legal ramifications. Courts to date, however, have not found a constitutional basis to force school boards to take affirmative action to correct racial imbalances not brought about by any of their prior actions. In some instances, however, judicial relief has been granted. These have been cases where staffs or facilities of predominantly Negro schools were markedly inferior, or where there could be applied a clear pupil assignment pattern which would bring about marked improvement in the racial compositions of the schools in a district without destroying over valued educational concepts.

A widely publicized example of court action came in 1967 in Washington, D.C. The school system had been using a "tracking" plan through which students were assigned to instructional programs early in their school careers based on scores achieved on tests. The tests were of doubtful validity for such purposes. Furthermore, it was very difficult for students once placed on a track to change tracks. An additional fact was that most "Negro and poor white students" were on the lower tracks. This system of assignment of pupils was invalidated by federal courts as being unconstitutionally discriminatory.

In the North and West there has been an emergence of legislation, administrative action, and quasi-judicial rulings by state-level educational authorities which have put upon school boards in states affected an affirmative duty to improve racial balances in public schools. State statutes requiring school boards to correct de facto segregation have been upheld as constitutional. So have actions of state boards of education and chief state school officers ordering that affirmative steps be taken by local boards. State-level educational authorities have passed regulations to this effect in some instances, and in others the impact has come from their quasi-judicial rulings. The courts tend to reason that assignments of pupils, teachers, and facilities are basically educational decisions, and that it is not the function of the courts to inquire into the social, philosophical, and educational bases of decisions made by educational authorities unless there is evidence of infringement of someone's rights or abuse of discretionary power. Thus, almost uniformly sustained by courts have been programs initiated by local boards of education to improve racial balance in the schools or otherwise to improve educational opportunities for all children.

Addendum

In late October of 1969 the Supreme Court unanimously ruled that "continued operation of segregated schools under a standard of allowing 'all deliberate speed' for desegregation is no longer constitutionally permissible. . . . The obligation of every school district is to terminate dual school systems at once and to operate now and hereafter only unitary schools." The case was an appeal from a lower court decision granting more time to some Mississippi school districts for desegregation.

Appendix A

Table I
METHOD OF SELECTION OF MAJORITY
OF MEMBERS OF
STATE BOARD OF EDUCATION

By Voters: Colorado, Connecticut, Georgia, Hawaii, Kansas, Louisiana, Michigan, Missouri, Nebraska, Nevada, New Mexico, Ohio, Texas, Utah

By Governor: Alabama, Alaska, Arizona, Arkansas, California, Delaware, Idaho, Indiana, Iowa, Kentucky, Maine, Maryland, Massachusetts, Minnesota, Montana, New Hampshire, New Jersey, North Carolina, Oklahoma, Oregon, Pennsylvania, Rhode Island, South Dakota, Tennessee, Vermont, Virginia, West Virginia.

Ex Officio: Florida, Mississippi, North Dakota

Other: New York, South Carolina, Washington, Wyoming

No State Board: Illinois, Wisconsin

Appendix B

Table II
METHOD OF SELECTION OF
CHIEF STATE SCHOOL OFFICER

By Voters: Alabama, Arizona, California, Florida, Georiga, Idaho, Illinois, Indiana, Kentucky, Louisiana, Mississippi, Montana, North Carolina, North Dakota, Oklahoma, Oregon, South Carolina, South Dakota, Washington, Wisconsin, Wyoming

By State Board of Education: Arkansas, Colorado, Connecticut, Delaware, Hawaii, Iowa, Kansas, Maine, Maryland, Massachusetts, Michigan, Minnesota, Missouri, Nebraska, Nevada, New Hampshire, New Mexico, New York, Ohio Rhode Island, Texas, Utah, Vermont, West Virginia

By Governor: Alaska, New Jersey, Pennsylvania, Tennessee, Virginia

Appendix C

Table III
METHOD OF SELECTION
OF LOCAL SCHOOL BOARD MEMBERS

All Elected: Alaska, Arizona, Arkansas, California, Colorado, Connecticut, Florida, Idaho, Illinois, Iowa, Kansas, Kentucky, Louisiana, Maine, Massachusetts, Michigan, Minnesota, Missouri, Nebraska, Nevada, New Hampshire, New Mexico, North Dakota, Ohio, Oklahoma, Oregon, Rhode Island, South Dakota, Texas, Utah, Vermont, Washington, West Virginia, Wyoming

Most Elected: Alabama, Delaware, Indiana, Mississippi, Montana, New Jersey, New York, Pennsylvania, Wisconsin

Elected Only Where Special Legislation Prevails: Georgia, Maryland, North Carolina, South Carolina, Tennsessee, Virginia

No Local Boards: Hawaii.

STATE OFFICES OF EDUCATION

Superintendent of Education
State Department of Education
Montgomery, Alabama 36104

Commissioner of Education
State Department of Education
Juneau, Alaska 99801

Superintendent of Public Instruction
State Department of Public Instruction
Phoenix, Arizona 85007

Commissioner of Education
State Department of Education
Little Rock, Arkansas 72201

Superintendent of Public Instruction
State Department of Education
Sacremento, California 95814

Commissioner of Education
State Department of Education
State Office Building
Denver, Colorado 80203

Commissioner of Education
State Department of Education
P.O. Box 2219
Hartford, Connecticut 06115

Superintendent of Public Instruction
State Department of Public Instruction
Dover, Delaware 19901

Superintendent of Public Instruction
State Department of Education
Tallahassee, Florida 32304

Superintendent of Schools
State Department of Education
Atlanta, Georgia 30334

Superintendent of Education
State Department of Education
Honolulu, Hawaii 96804

Superintendent of Public Instruction
State Department of Education
Boise, Idaho 83702

Superintendent of Public Instruction
Office of the Superintendent of Public Instruction
302 State Office Building
Springfield, Illinois 62706

Superintendent of Public Instruction
State Department of Public Instruction
Indianapolis, Indiana 46204

Superintendent of Public Instruction
State Department of Public Instruction
Des Moines, Iowa 50319

Superintendent of Public Instruction
State Department of Public Instruction
Topeka, Kansas 66612

Superintendent of Public Instruction
State Department of Education
Frankfort, Kentucky 40601

Superintendent of Public Education
State Department of Education
Baton Rouge, Louisiana 70804

Commissioner of Education
State Department of Education
Augusta, Maine 04330

Superintendent of Schools
State Department of Education
Baltimore, Maryland 21201

Commissioner of Education
State Department of Education
Boston, Massachusetts 02111

Superintendent of Public Instruction
State Department of Education
Lansing, Michigan 48902

Commissioner of Education
State Department of Education
St. Paul, Minnesota 55101

Superintendent of Public Education
State Department of Education
Jackson, Mississippi 39205

Commissioner of Education
State Department of Education
Jefferson City, Missouri 65101

Superintendent of Public Instruction
State Department of Public Instruction
Helena, Montana 59601

Commissioner of Education
State Department of Education
Lincoln, Nebraska 68509

Superintendent of Public Instruction
State Department of Education
Carson City, Nevada 89701

Commissioner of Education
State Department of Education
Concord, New Hampshire 03301

Commissioner of Education
State Department of Education
Trenton, New Jersey 08625

Superintendent of Public Instruction
State Department of Education
Santa Fe, New Mexico 87501

Commissioner of Education
State Education Department
Albany, New York 12224

Superintendent of Public Instruction
State Board of Education
Raleigh, North Carolina 27602

Superintendent of Public Instruction
State Department of Public Instruction
Bismarck, North Dakota 58501

Superintendent of Public Instruction
State Department of Education
Ohio Departments Building
Columbus, Ohio 43215

Superintendent of Public Instruction
State Department of Education
Oklahoma City, Oklahoma 73105

Superintendent of Public Instruction
State Department of Education
Salem, Oregon 97310

Superintendent of Public Instruction
State Department of Public Instruction
Harrisburg, Pennsylvania 17126

Commissioner of Education
State Department of Education
Providence, Rhode Island 02908

Superintendent of Education
State Department of Education
Columbia, South Carolina 29201

Superintendent of Public Instruction
State Department of Public Instruction
Pierre, South Dakota 57501

Commissioner of Education
State Department of Education
Nashville, Tennessee 37219

Commissioner of Education
Texas Education Agency
Austin, Texas 78711

Superintendent of Public Instruction
Office of the Superintendent
Salt Lake City, Utah 84111

Commissioner of Education
State Department of Education
Montpelier, Vermont 05602

Superintendent of Public Instruction
State Board of Education
Richmond, Virginia 23216

Superintendent of Public Instruction
Office of State Superintendent of Public Instruction
Olympia, Washington 98501

Superintendent of Schools
State Department of Education
Charleston, West Virginia 25305

Superintendent of Public Instruction
State Department of Public Instruction
126 Langdon Street
Madison, Wisconsin 53702

Superintendent of Public Instruction
State Department of Education
Cheyenne, Wyoming 82001

Secretary of Education
Department of Education
Hato Rey, Puerto Rico 00919

INDEX

LEGAL ALMANAC SERIES

LAW FOR THE LAYMAN—COVERS ALL STATES

Price Per Volume: $3.00, $3.50 for No. 9

**Oceana Publications, Inc.
Dobbs Ferry, N.Y. 10522**